CW00348883

Imbolc

The Ultimate Guide to Brigid, and Candlemas and How It's Celebrated in Christianity, Wicca, Druidry, and Celtic paganism

Your Free Gift (only available for a limited time)

Thanks for getting this book! If you want to learn more about various spirituality topics, then join Mari Silva's community and get a free guided meditation MP3 for awakening your third eye. This guided meditation mp3 is designed to open and strengthen ones third eye so you can experience a higher state of consciousness. Simply visit the link below the image to get started.

https://spiritualityspot.com/meditation

Table of Contents

Introduction

The desire to celebrate Imbolc is one of the purest. It's not ego-based or rooted in a desire to become more interesting or attract more attention when speaking to people. It's rooted in a genuine connection to nature, Brigid, or both. It's also an act that is rooted in love. Without this level of authenticity, all we get is another empty tradition void of meaning.

When reading about Imbolc (or other pagan festivals, concepts, deities, and other studies like astrology and numerology), we often notice hints toward subjective misinformation, either intentional or not.

For one, it's really hard to find credible sources, and, in almost all cases, it takes a seasoned practitioner to provide guidance and source references. Otherwise, it's a process of trial and error. Especially when it comes to spirituality, this can be exhausting if not dangerous.

It's also hard to pinpoint one's intention from their writing. Some authors don't care about those who read their books and blogs. They may omit or cherry-pick information to appeal to the readers. They may also be using paganism to glorify themselves, which is one of the factors behind misinformation.

On the other side of the coin, there are many old-school authors able to provide a treasure trove of information. However, they tend to miss the mark when explaining rituals and spells because of the inaccessible ingredients many of them use.

Then, there are the authors who speak about spirituality from their perspectives, which, of course, is appreciated. Nevertheless, it can alienate many who don't view things in the same light or who don't connect to the same deities, herbs, plants, and rituals as they do, which creates the false belief that the spiritual journey is a straight line with strict practices. It divides the pagans who practice "right" and those who practice "wrong."

These issues are exactly what we do our best to avoid in this book. Rather than get caught up with what's on the surface of Imbolc practices, we delve deep into what this early spring festival is about. After fleshing it out, we take each aspect of the festival, from its associated herbs to the crafts and spells. That way, we give each part of Imbolc the attention it deserves.

More importantly, because we understand how complex spirituality is, we made sure we have provided enough alternatives so everyone can find something with which they connect. What one person may feel called to do may not be how others feel, and this is the approach we will be taking throughout this book.

Before we start, you're invited to keep your mind and heart open to what your instincts and your guides communicate to you throughout the book. Remember that the universe communicates with us in the most subtle things and the most mundane ways.

Now, without further ado, let's start down the path to explore this beautiful festival and everything it stands for.

Chapter 1: Introduction to Imbolc

Imbolc celebration.
steven earnshaw, CC BY 2.0 <https://creativecommons.org/licenses/by/2.0>, via Wikimedia Commons: https://commons.wikimedia.org/wiki/File:Imbolc_Festival_February_3rd_2007.jpg

Imbolc is a significant pagan festival heavily rooted in ancient Celtic culture. While nowadays, it's more commonly known as St. Brigid's Day and is also celebrated as a Christian holiday. The origins of this holiday go back to pre-Christian Ireland, Scotland,

and the Isle of Man.

The pagan Wheel of the Year consists of eight seasonal festivals. Four of these festivals occur on the two solstices and the two equinoxes. These four events mark the beginnings of the four seasons based on the position of the Earth from the sun:

- Yule is celebrated with the winter solstice on 21st December.
- Ostara is celebrated with the spring equinox on 20th March.
- Litha is celebrated with the summer solstice on 21st June.
- Mabon is celebrated with the autumn equinox on 22nd September.

Meanwhile, the other four festivals are called cross-quarter days and occur between the four main festivals or sabbats. These are:

- Imbolc - celebrated on 1st February between Yule and Ostara.
- Beltane - celebrated on 1st May between Ostara and Litha.
- Lughnasadh - celebrated on 1st August between Litha and Mabon.
- Samhain - celebrated on 31st October and 1st November between Mabon and Yule.

Because it's celebrated on the 1st of February, between the winter solstice and the spring equinox, Imbolc represents the "coming" of spring. It's the time of the year during the tail end of winter when people start to notice signs of the coming of spring.

Of course, after a cold and hard winter where the nights reached their darkest, the days their shortest, and life was made dim by the cold, the signs of spring are more than worthy of celebration. It was especially so in the distant past when people depended directly on the seasons to plant or hunt, and this festival was held in very high regard.

Imbolc's Cultural Significance

The culture that ruled pre-Christian Ireland, Scotland, and the Isle of Man was mainly farming-oriented. The lands had plenty of greenery and fertile soil, so farming was the easiest way to sustain life and make money. Of course, certain birds, animals, and cattle came with farming.

In winter, the world naturally grows cold. This means that, for any warm-blooded creature to survive, their bodies need to exert extra effort to maintain their blood temperature at a reasonable level. The stronger winter gets, the harder it is for animals to maintain their temperature.

All warm-blooded creatures try to find ways to cope with this great inconvenience. Some animals migrate to a warm place because life becomes too unsuitable for them. Others hibernate to avoid dealing with the temperature difference, and others decrease their activity levels to conserve their resources.

The same goes for plants. The plants' enzymes don't function well in cold temperatures. And, because a decrease in temperature means slower movements on an atomic level, roots don't absorb nutrient particles as efficiently. So, instead of wasting their energy making new leaves, plants shut down photosynthesis and dedicate all their resources to survival.

As you see, in winter, the world becomes an inhospitable place for the warm-blooded. It's a time to survive rather than thrive. Nevertheless, this difficult time and the collective human despair and frustration that come with it usually end with the promise of spring. This is where Imbolc draws its cultural significance.

On Imbolc, the whole community would celebrate that the time to survive was coming to an end. They no longer needed to store or conserve food, and they didn't have to worry for their lives. Plants start growing their leaves around that time, so it's a sign that Mother Earth's womb is ready to receive and produce seeds.

In addition to that, animals are nearing their last months of hibernation. And some animals even give birth around or shortly after this time because it is when a newborn can tolerate the weather.

With all of that being said, it's obvious why everyone used to come together to celebrate this particular day. It's also obvious why festivals had very significant roles back then. They often coincided with agricultural events that affected the region as a whole. So, regardless of one's religion or beliefs, they all had the same core reason to celebrate.

Imbolc's Historical Significance

If you take a look at Celtic sagas and mythologies, you'll be able to see the influence of the rural culture. Among the most glorified creatures in Irish mythology were two in particular; Glas Gaibhnenn, a cow that produced near-infinite amounts of milk, and Manannan mac Lir's immortal swine, which always came alive the next morning after it had been killed.

Both reflected the wishes of kings and commoners alike and reflected how deeply people valued these specific animals; the well-fed swine and the cow that produces plenty of milk. Because the grass grows faster in spring, cows produce the most milk in spring (milking season), and pigs gain the most weight. Because Imbolc was associated with fertility, growth, and regeneration, it gained a lot of historical significance.

The legendary Hill of Tara, where the stone of destiny, Lia Fáil, stands, was and is a sacred historical location according to Irish tradition. In close proximity to it lies a burial mound called the "Mound of Hostages."

The entrance to the Mound of Hostages is positioned so that it would be in alignment with the sun on two occasions; Imbolc and Samhain. At the start of the two festivals, the sunlight makes its way through the entrance and to an engraved stone at the back of the chamber and then lights it up for about a week.

Imbolc's Spiritual Significance

Culture and history aside, Imbolc has a strong spiritual significance for all pagans. One of the pillars of paganism is one's connectedness to nature and the earth, which is one of several reasons the eight festivals on the Wheel of the Year were created. They were ways for the first worshippers to tune into the Earth's cycle around the sun and its effects on all life forms and forces.

Another reason was that Imbolc was a spiritual event worthy of celebration. As the Earth orbits the sun, the land reaches a point farthest from the planet's main source of energy and life. On a physical level, this natural phenomenon creates the winter season.

This phenomenon stands for darkness and death on a mental and spiritual level. This is not necessarily an evil type of darkness and death but the natural end of a cycle and the natural opposition to light and life. It's a time to rest and work on shedding harmful behaviors and thoughts.

It can also be a time of deep depression and frustration as we lose touch with our light source. On a biological and chemical level, this can cause vitamin D deficiency and trigger seasonal affective disorder where the individual experiences depression-like symptoms.

This disconnection from the fire element can trigger a decline in one's energy and passion on a spiritual level. It can manifest in a loss of joy and passion, a lack of ambitions and motivation, and a decline in libido (sex drive).

All in all, it doesn't sound like a great time. Granted, it can be beneficial for some people as it can push repressed emotions and trauma to the surface so they can be released. However, that doesn't mean that winter is only a tough and joyless time.

This is why, as it nears its end, we celebrate Imbolc. After such an intense season where people have gone through the process of shedding beliefs, processing trauma, and grieving losses and absences, it's only fair to celebrate that we have made it through. Not just that, but it also makes sense to celebrate the coming season, the return of the light, and the rekindling of the fire within us. This is also why Imbolc is considered one of the four fire festivals.

Celebrating Imbolc marks this wonderful beginning of a new cycle. It allows us to reflect on the past and set intentions and hopes for the future. It also allows us to cleanse ourselves and our surroundings and let go of everything we wish to leave behind. That way, we can wholly embrace the new cycle in a much better way.

Not just that, but celebrating such a day allows individuals to deepen their connection to the cycle that influences us and rules the elements around and within us. This brings a deeper sense of spiritual alignment and allows people to make the most out of each phase and its influences.

One can start planting seeds for new thoughts and behaviors on this day. It's also when they can start acting on their New Year's resolutions or planning for them. We all make the mistake of holding ourselves to our resolutions while forgetting that winter is not the time to grow anything.

Each year, the fact that we get to celebrate Imbolc presents us with the promise that there will come a time when we feel energized and motivated to act. It's a comforting message, especially for those who can't stay still or don't feel comfortable losing their motivation. It's a message from nature that says, "There is a time for everything. Don't worry. It wasn't yet your time to move forward, but it will soon be."

For Wiccans, Imbolc holds an almost identical, albeit slightly different, significance. In addition to everything mentioned above, Imbolc represents the transformation or the role shift that the Goddess goes through.

The Goddess is a Wiccan triple deity who takes on three forms; the Maiden, the Mother, and the Crone. Each represents certain aspects of female energy and expresses the divine feminine.

The Crone is the form that the Goddess takes during wintertime. It's her elder aspect that brings forth wisdom and represents death. At the same time, it represents rebirth and transformation as the Crone is reborn into the Maiden at the start of spring.

Imbolc is also considered a celebration of this transformation. It takes time to reflect on the wisdom attained during the past year. And, just like the Crone gracefully embraces her rebirth as the Maiden, Imbolc presents an opportunity to become humble and open oneself up to the new cycle.

The Festival's Etymology

Imbolc is a variation of the Old Irish words "*i mbolg*," which, when translated, means "in the womb."

Now, the name is part-metaphorical and part-literal.

As we've mentioned, Imbolc marks the start of spring. It marks a time when life and warmth are just returning to the Earth. The living conditions are just starting to become suitable enough for animals and birds to give birth to their babies. We should also mention that people take this time to prepare for sowing their seeds. This is the literal part as, during this time, seeds are planted in the womb of the Earth. Animals, too, start to reach the peak of their development inside their mothers' wombs before coming out into the world during springtime.

As for the symbolic part, what's signified by the womb is the beginning of life. In the winter season, trees stop growing leaves, animals hibernate, many crops go out of season, and people refrain from making much effort to preserve their energy. The pace of life significantly slows down. Imbolc marks the time when the wheels of life start to move again, when the Earth as a whole begins to, once again, wake up and rejuvenate itself.

This is what Imbolc celebrated and still celebrates. Although, between back then and nowadays, there are a few differences in how people approach the festival.

Imbolc in the Past

One fundamental difference that separates how people used to celebrate Imbolc in the past from how they do now is in their connectedness to nature.

In the past, we were almost at one with nature. There was nothing separating people from their surroundings. People lived on the land and from the animals they had. There weren't as many divisions or layers between them and nature as there are now with corporations, mass production, etc.

People were also at the mercy of the elements. The sun was their main source of light. Meanwhile, nowadays, we might turn on the lights when it gets too cloudy outside. And, if you get cold in your insulated house or apartment, imagine how cold it was inside a clay/wooden house and under a straw ceiling.

This is why, back then, more and more people celebrated the festival. Not only did it impact pagans on a spiritual level, but it impacted everyone on all levels. They rejoiced that soon there was going to be plenty of food, that the nights were only going to get warmer until Samhain, and that the light would get brighter.

As a result of the festival's national presence, it was customary for people to gather around huge bonfires, feast, and dance. It was a way of further summoning the light and awakening the dormant fire element. At the same time, it celebrated the end of winter.

Among the other traditions observed by the public was the preparation of the land so that, come springtime, it would be ready for planting. Around this time, it was also common to see people doing their share of spring cleaning around their houses to prepare for the new year.

People would also visit holy wells, pray for fertility, health, and blessings for the new year and leave offerings for the gods. Water from these wells was considered holy and taken home as a source of blessings for the house and whoever drank it.

Last but not least, people also used to pour milk and porridge into the rivers and seas or the ground as an offering to the gods and goddesses of nature and fertility.

Imbolc Is the Present

Nowadays, what's common isn't a connection to nature but a disconnection. So, for one person to have this connection, they must have worked to nurture and maintain it. Imbolc has lost its popularity the more advanced our way of life has become.

It's reached the point where the only people who celebrate Imbolc are pagans and Wiccans. Of course, there are Christians who celebrate St. Brigid's day, but while it takes place on Imbolc, it's not entirely the same.

From a purely pagan lens, the traditions associated with Imbolc have undergone a great shift from the physical to the mental and spiritual. Instead of preparing the land, people take this time to cleanse their bodies, houses, minds, and spirits. Instead of planting seeds, people take the time to meditate on or journal about the ideas, projects, beliefs, thoughts, etc., that they'd like to plant within themselves.

Some people take the time to plan for their New Year's resolutions, and others even skip New Year's and make their resolutions on Imbolc.

Nevertheless, the core concepts remain unchanged even with the differences, and it shows primarily in the symbols. People drink and eat milk and baked goods on Imbolc to celebrate the milking season. They light bonfires and candles to invoke the fire element within themselves and celebrate the sun's return.

People also prepare food to special recipes for an Imbolc feast and come together to recite poems and prayers. On the one hand, it's a celebration of the coming of light and spring. On the other hand, it's a tradition that allows people to reflect on the past and let go of any baggage that may hold them back.

Last but not least, Imbolc is one of the ways for modern pagans to nurture their connection with Mother Nature and attune themselves to its cycle.

Imbolc and Current Associations

The Imbolc Festival has many associations, whether with symbols, colors, herbs, deities, tools, crystals, or animals. Throughout this book, we will discuss them in detail, but giving you a roadmap, here are the most prominent things linked to Imbolc.

Symbols

- Brigid's Cross
- Brigid Doll
- Milk
- Baked goods
- Snowdrop flowers
- Fire
- Candles

Colors

- Red
- Orange
- White
- Green

Deities

- Brigid
- The Wiccan Goddess

Herbs and Plants

- Bay Leaves
- Heather
- Rosemary
- Angelica
- Basil

Tools

- Hearths
- Bonfires
- Altars
- Special offerings

Crystals/Stones

- Amethyst
- Sunstone
- Peridot

Animals

- Cows
- Sheep

Having named these items, you need to remember that everything is highly subjective, especially when it comes to spirituality. You may feel drawn to certain items not mentioned within this book, and that's okay. In fact, you should welcome that.

Many of us prefer to use herbs other than rosemary for their cleansing effects. Meanwhile, some people can just be drawn to particular stones and crystals as they embark on a new cycle. This freedom, openness, and harmony are all about the spiritual experience.

More importantly, it's an incredibly personal and diverse experience. Rules or pre-appointed symbols cannot control our souls and how we relate to the spiritual. So, keep your mind and heart open to how you feel as you read on. Do what feels right to you, and remember that nothing is set in stone.

Chapter 2: Brigid, Goddess, and Saint

Earlier in the previous chapter, we mentioned that Imbolc is also called St. Brigid's Day. Then we said that they were not entirely the same. Now is the time to expand on both statements.

Imbolc is the time and festival in which pagans also celebrate the Irish goddess Brigid. Not only is she seen as a goddess of fire and a herald of spring, but she's also a triple goddess with a maiden aspect that shines at the beginning of the yearly cycle.

When Christianity came to Ireland and the surrounding countries, the missionaries declared Brigid a saint. It was an attempt to gain the favor of the local population while making their transition to Christianity easier and smoother by including a familiar face.

It is, however, important to say that some scholars genuinely believe that St. Brigid bore no relationship to the goddess. Instead, they think she was an abbess (Mother Superior) who was granted sainthood after managing to found a convent of nuns in Kildare.

As a pagan celebrating Imbolc, whether you're focused on the nature-related, spiritual, or divine aspects of the day, the foundation of your rituals and traditions will be somewhat the same. That's why interchangeability is acceptable here.

However, as a Christian celebrating St. Brigid's Day, your rituals' intentions and foundation will differ, even if your traditions share similarities with pagan ones. This is why we maintain that Imbolc and St. Brigid's Day are not entirely the same.

In Imbolc, Brigid is a central figure to the pagans who choose to worship and revere gods. Not all pagans worship the gods. Some are simply animists who believe that all things have spirits and an influence on humans. As we said before, there is no gate-keeping when it comes to spirituality. It's all about what we feel drawn toward.

For those who feel drawn toward Brigid on this day, it's because of the goddess's captivating identity.

Brigid

In Irish mythology, Brigid was the daughter of the Dagda (the father god of all Irish deities) and The Morrigan (the triple goddess of war). In addition to her unique identity, many of her qualities were shaped by her parents, their abilities, and their characteristics.

Brigid is known first and foremost as a goddess of poetry and wisdom. Being also a goddess of healing and the daughter of an all-father, she is an advocate for peace. In her stories, she married Bres simply to keep the peace between the gods and a race of giants.

However, as much as she's willing to do for peace, she can prove to be a fearsome warrior if need be. After all, she was the daughter of the Morrigan. Brigid also draws her protective instincts from her mother, which fuels her reputation as the guardian and protector of women in combination with her feminine side.

Brigid plays a central role for more than one reason when it comes to Imbolc. First of all, she is a fire goddess and brings warmth after the cold months of winter. Secondly, she's associated with fertility in women and crops. People even used to invoke her name when they needed their cows to produce milk. Thirdly, wherever she travels, she travels with Glas Gaibhnenn, the sacred cow that produces infinite amounts of milk.

Spring is a celebration of fertility. Animals give birth and produce milk. Famines end as seeds turn to plants, and plants grow lush leaves full of life. Poems are sung in celebration, as warmth and new birth return to the Earth. And so, Imbolc is the day to invoke Brigid, the one goddess associated with all it is that makes up spring.

Nevertheless, this is not all there is to Brigid. This triple goddess is a complex entity with multiple aspects and associations. Understanding her relationship with Imbolc and how to honor her during this time is crucial to understanding who she is. More importantly, don't forget to reflect on what you learn, so you can understand who she is to you.

The Triple Goddess

The most important part of Brigid's identity is her three-fold form. Each of her aspects presents a different side of her. And each trinity represents a different part of Brigid's identity.

First off, Brigid's not only a goddess of poetry but also a goddess of healing and a goddess of smithing. She floats between these three forms, exalting one at a time but housing all of them at all times.

Second, Brigid is often illustrated as holding fire in her hand. It's an expression of her being a fire goddess and a bringer of light. In alignment with her three-fold form, she represents the three fires:

- The fire of the hearth represents fertility, a warm and blessed home, and healing.

- The fire of the forge stands for crafting and smithing.

- The fire of inspiration represents her wisdom and identity as a poet and an inspiration for wise men and poets.

This is why the physical representation of Brigid's complex character is fire. It's also why people often burn fires for Brigid to invoke her spirit and her blessings.

In the past, a burning hearth was at the center of every house, spreading warmth to the people who lived in the house. The people who put time and effort into tending the fire were a manifestation of that love. And travelers who, from afar, saw a hearth fire burning inside a house were filled with a sense of hope and relief. They also knew that whoever was inside would offer them food and a place to stay. This was healing after a long journey, just as warmth is healing after a long winter.

Once again, Brigid's warmth, love, healing, hope, and relief are all associated with what Imbolc gives us, from the promise of light to the bounties that come with the season.

The Goddess of Poetry

Brigid, the goddess of poetry and inspiration, offers us herself as a muse during Imbolc. Inspiration is the seed of poetry, but one has to start with a blank page to create. Similarly, to think clearly and prepare for new experiences, you need to let go of old influences, outdated perceptions, and other forms of baggage; only then can you truly get the most out of it.

After a long winter filled with demotivation, a lack of inspiration, and sluggish energy, the coming of the sun and Brigid's fire of inspiration give us a much-needed push into the opening world of a new season. Spring is the perfect time to connect with Brigid, ask for her blessings, and receive her energy. It's the best time to give birth to new ideas because this is when the mind is as fertile as the Earth.

So, don't hesitate to start creating, planning, or taking action. Your decisions will see fruition as Brigid's fire of inspiration glows brighter, chasing away winter.

The Goddess of Healing

Fire represents purification and healing. It's a symbol of the sun and the coming of spring. Brigid is the goddess to which you can connect when you want to heal after grieving during winter. She's also there to help you purify, cleanse, and ready yourself for the new year cycle.

Because of her ability to heal illnesses and cleanse, Brigid is also associated with the element of water. Whether you take water from her wells or charge a coin with your intentions and throw it inside as an offering, you'll receive her blessings and healing.

The Goddess of Smithing

Brigid's third aspect and form are her as a goddess of smithing and the forge's fire. She's an inspiration, a muse, and a source of strength to creatives and crafters.

One of Brigid's first inventions was the whistle. It was a magical whistle designed to be used at night. It made a noise so loud that it drew people towards the whistleblower. It was her contribution to protecting women from assault.

Her energy and influence emanate through fire, and it's common to feel more driven and inspired as spring draws near. What's more, you won't meet as much resistance by starting your projects or working with the goddess during this time. In fact, you won't feel like you're working against the grain at all. Your ideas will flow, and crafting will be a joy, not a burden.

The Maiden

The goddess Brigid is known for her love, compassion, and generosity. In the past, pagans believed that life followed her everywhere she went - that flowers sprung under her feet and trees bore fruit at her touch. She is a fearless young goddess who brings life and healing everywhere she goes. With unquenchable fire as her element, no wonder Brigid was immediately associated with spring and birth.

One aspect of Brigid was her identity as a maiden. Using the Wiccan perspective as an example, let's say that Imbolc and spring are the beginning of life. They resemble a youthful maiden.

Summer resembles the maternal aspect of the divine feminine, the matron or the mother. After all, it is the lushest time of the year when there's plenty of everything, from crops, fruits, and flowers to animals.

Meanwhile, winter resembles the crone or the hag – the wise old lady who has lived a lifetime and is dying. She grieves her own death and sheds her current identity to prepare for rebirth with the coming of spring.

Cailleach is the ancient crone associated with and accredited with creating winter and landscapes in ancient Gaelic myths.

Cailleach was a giantess with a staff that froze the ground it touched and formed mountains when she accidentally dropped some rocks from her basket. She was the one who collected the clouds and covered the Earth with snow.

Cailleach ruled the winter months while Brigid ruled the summer months. At the end of winter, the crone turned herself into a stone pillar and made way for Brigid and the new life that came with her.

While the winter months bring to us destruction, the promise of Brigid's return brings a sense of warmth and hope. Around Imbolc, we start seeing signs of Brigid's return: blooming flowers (especially snowdrops), warmer nights, longer days, singing birds, and bumblebees.

Brigid's return also reminds us that death, depression, and loss don't last forever. New life always grows back.

Imbolc is also a great time for women and men to connect with the divine feminine through Brigid the maiden. It's a time to connect with her love, compassion, and powerful life force. Of course, one can also turn to the goddess for their mother and crone needs. However, during this time, Brigid's maiden aspect is at its peak.

The Saint and the Sacred Flame

A girl was born to a Druid father and a Christian mother one day. Her name was Brigid, and, like her father, she was dedicated to the worship of the Irish gods. However, she dedicated her life to honoring her namesake, Brigid, at a young age.

On the hill in Kildare, it was said that she gathered a group of nineteen priestesses, and, together, they kept a hearth fire burning to honor the goddess. Brigid then created this sisterhood which tended the goddess's fire, keeping it lit until the sixteenth century.

This fire was known as the sacred flame. It stayed alight, invoking Brigid's presence and spreading her blessings all over Earth as long as it remained.

When St. Patrick came into Ireland and proceeded to spread Christianity throughout the land, Brigid's mother invited him to talk to Brigid. Eventually, he convinced her to become Christian, and she dedicated her life to Christianity.

She started a convent in Kildare, where she used to tend the fire and, even there, she still kept the fire burning. As time passed, the Catholic Church's hold grew strong enough for the pope to order a full transition from paganism to Christianity.

The sacred flame was extinguished when pagan temples and artifacts were shut down and destroyed. Then, it was re-lit in 1993 in the market square in Kildare by the Brigidine Sisters. Brigid's fire is still tended until now in a place of worship called Solas Bhirde, Kildare, Ireland.

This is the story of Brigid and the sacred flame, which became a form of veneration and worship practiced by all of the goddess's followers. However, there are several theories about who Brigid, the human, was.

Because Brigid, the goddess, could shapeshift and assume different forms, it's believed that she was St. Brigid, except that, back then, she transformed herself into a little girl who grew up to be a saint. It was all because her people needed her to appear in this form at the time, like when she assumed the form of Maman Brigitte for her people who moved to Haiti and the Caribbean Islands to fit with their needs.

Had she retained the identity of Brigid, the goddess, her people would not have been able to practice her worship or feel her influence. It was illegal to practice any form of pagan worship or celebrate any pagan festivals. However, once Brigid had taken a saint form, she became accessible to her people again.

Not only that, but she became accessible to everyone who believed in St. Brigid, Christians and pagans alike. It's only fitting to reiterate what we said at the beginning of the chapter: Brigid is a complex goddess.

The last theory developed by scholars was about Christianity merging the Irish goddess and everything that represented her with Christian imagery. It was a common method used by the Catholic Church throughout Europe and Scandinavia.

Maman Brigitte

Another facet of Brigid's identity is the death loa, Maman Brigitte.

Maman Brigitte is a spirit in Haitian Vodou religion. When the New World was created, many Irish, English, and Scottish people - women in particular - entered into indentured servitude contracts.

This type of slavery was based on the barter system. The wealthy offered to pay the travel costs for the poor who wanted to migrate to the New World. Those people would work as enslaved people for the rich for a specified time.

As the Celtic peoples migrated to the Caribbean Islands and Haiti, they brought with them their traditions. Because most were women, they brought Brigid Dolls as a protection charm with them. After all, Brigid is the protector of women.

This was how Brigid, the Irish goddess, adopted a new aspect, Maman Brigitte, the death loa.

In Haitian Vodou, a loa is a spirit. Maman Brigitte is the Haitian death spirit primarily associated with guardianship and cemeteries. Back then, she was believed to live in the trees within graveyards, and she was invoked for multiple reasons.

Similar to Brigid, Maman Brigitte was a protector and a deliverer of punishment when the need arose. She was invoked when a woman needed to get justice but was unable to because the law didn't favor her. When it came to punishment, Maman Brigitte was a spirit to be feared. Given that historical time period, she was an ancient symbol of female empowerment.

She was also called upon by families who wanted her to protect their kin fighting wars abroad. She was also invoked whenever someone needed healing. Because Maman Brigitte was a great healer, she was the spirit people depended upon when they were desperate. They knew that she would step in and either heal the sick or relieve them by making their death a painless one.

Maman Brigitte is heavily associated with the fire element like her Irish counterpart. People worship and honor her using blue and purple candles, as these are her colors. And, according to tradition, she appreciates offerings of extremely hot peppers, especially when steeped in a glass or container of rum.

During the time of Imbolc, if you feel drawn to work with Maman Brigitte, you'll get the best results if the intent of your magic is oriented towards:

- Love

Whether it is romantic love, passion, connection, or communication, Maman Brigitte's energy and influence can be strong in these matters specifically, as this is her time of blooming.

- **Authority**

Maman Brigitte is a dominant figure and one of authority. She commands death and bestows punishment as she sees fit. She can help when it comes to matters of authority, power, control, and developing self-confidence.

- **Fire**

Any magical workings related to fire will be exalted during the time of Imbolc. Some people choose to practice divination with fire, while others practice fire scrying. Both are very good methods to connect with Maman Brigitte's influence.

- **Healing**

There is none other than Maman Brigitte to resort to when it comes to health, protection, and fertility. She is the protector of women, the commander of death, and a master healer.

Can you see the similarities between Brigid and Maman Brigitte? It is believed that Brigid saw that, at the time, her people needed her protection and guidance as they were enslaved in foreign lands. However, they needed it in a particular form, so she took on the form of Maman Brigitte.

On Imbolc, we celebrate Brigid with all her aspects, facets, and forms - her entire complex identity. Because she is a fire goddess associated with light, life, and healing, we focus on her during the coming of spring. We honor her, express our gratitude, and allow her exalted influence to impact our lives where we most need it.

Chapter 3: Candlemas and Imbolc

Candlemas is a Christian festival also celebrated on the 2nd of February. It's known as the feast of the presentation of Jesus Christ. It's also known as the feast of the purification of the Blessed Virgin Mary. Meanwhile, in French, it's referred to as Chandeleur, which comes from the word "*chandelle*," meaning candle. Also, it's alternatively known as *la fête de la lumière*" or the festival of lights.

As you can see from some of these names, this festival is also associated with light, purification, new beginnings, and the element of fire which, in a way, makes it almost the same as Imbolc or St. Brigid's day. However, the jury is still out on whether they are the same holiday.

There are various opinions about the matter. Some people believe that Candlemas and Imbolc are different names for the same holiday. Others believe that they're different holidays. Meanwhile, some people argue that it's a Catholic adaptation of a pagan holiday.

Who is right? There's no telling. And not only that, but it's also not important. At the end of the day, what makes a festival are the intentions of the ones celebrating. However, what is important is understanding where the various opinions come from.

This chapter will discuss the differences between Candlemas and Imbolc and the complete Christian origins and traditions of Candlemas. So, if you feel you want to form an opinion on the matter or feel you're a little bit curious, this chapter will answer all your questions. It may even add a little bit of depth to how you celebrate Imbolc and inspire you to adopt a specific tradition.

Candlemas for Christians

Before we delve into the debate of whether or not Candlemass is Imbolc, we need to understand everything about Candlemas, its meaning, and its significance in Christianity.

Understanding the significance of Candlemas is no simple matter because many names know it, and each name highlights a different aspect of the celebration.

The Feast of the Presentation of Jesus Christ

You should remember this event from Jesus Christ's childhood if you're familiar with the Bible.

Forty days after Jesus was born, he was taken by Mary and Joseph to a temple in Jerusalem.

According to the Laws of Moses, if the firstborn child was a male, he should be presented and dedicated to God and give a sacrifice. The sacrifice consisted of a pair of doves or pigeons.

The origins of the law go back to when Moses was leading the Israelites out of Egypt. Exodus 13:2 says, "*Consecrate to me every firstborn male. The first offspring of every womb among the Israelites belongs to me, whether human or animal.*"

And this is what Mary and Joseph did. They took their firstborn to the temple to dedicate him and his life to God's service. More than that, however, Jesus was the son of God, and he came to Earth to save his people. So, his coming to the temple was not just a passive action following an ancient tradition.

Jesus's birth represented the arrival of the Savior on Earth. His coming to the temple was a confirmation of the fact that things were about to change. It was the first step that set many events in motion. In a way, the child had connected with his life path and was set on it.

So, one significant aspect of Candlemas is the celebration of the beginning of a life in the service of God. This aspect, however, is four-fold. It was a celebration of the start of Jesus's journey to serve God, which ended with him dying on the cross to save mankind. Two, it's a day for Christians to remember to dedicate their lives and focus on God rather than the material world. Three, it's an opportunity to act on this remembrance and either start the journey or get back on track.

Four, the church is often regarded as a mother in the eyes of its people, given its role in nurturing, guiding, and providing safety. Ephesians 5:25, *"Husbands, love your wives, as Christ loved the church and gave himself up for her,"* is only one verse where the church is personified as a wife and a mother.

Just like Mary, the mother, came to the temple to present her child, so did the church during this time. A church regards that day as one to call upon its people and present them to their service to God.

The Feast of the Purification of the Blessed Virgin Mary

Another Law of Moses that the Israelites observed is mentioned in Leviticus 12:2, "A *woman who becomes pregnant and gives birth to a son will be ceremonially unclean for seven days...*"

After seven days of giving birth to a male, the woman was to soak in water to purify herself. Then, she was to wait for 33 days. She couldn't worship, touch anything sacred, or visit a temple in those days. This period was called a "purification period," it doubled if the child was a girl (14 days before soaking in water and a 66-day purification period afterward).

When this purification period was over, the woman had to take a year-old lamb and a pigeon or a dove to a priest so he could sacrifice them on her behalf. The lamb was to be given as a burnt offering, a general sacrifice, and a sign of her devotion to god. The pigeon was to be given as a sin offering.

Jewish and Christian teachings refer to birth as a process where a mother creates life while staring death in the face. She endures a great deal of pain and suffering, which, on many occasions, ends with joy and relief. However, there is still the possibility of other outcomes.

According to Christian and Jewish beliefs, when individuals have made close contact with death, they need to go through a purification process. The ritual, which includes cleansing, a waiting period, and a sacrifice, is intended to purify the mother and connect her to life and God.

When Mary and Joseph took Jesus to the temple, it was 40 days after his birth which meant it was after Mary's purification period was over. At the time, she also had to offer her sacrifices to God to undo her separation from the living world.

This is why the feast is taken as a time to celebrate the Virgin Mary and her purification. Not only that, but it also is considered by the church a time for purification. Before giving one's life to God, a person needs to be pure from sin. They need to recover from the separation that being away from God causes and connect to him. The church considers this an opportunity to encourage its people to purify themselves.

The Festival of Light

John 8:12 goes, *"Jesus spoke to them, saying, 'I am the world's light.'"*. You can already see where the symbolism originates. Now, let's consider what candles represented in ancient times.

We've already discussed how the sun was the main source of light, only replaced by hearth fires or candles. In the wintertime, when nights were long, the fire was what people depended on to see and to work.

Candles gave people hope. Sometimes they helped guide travelers and gatekeepers and provided a sense of safety in the darkest of times.

Because Candlemas is a celebration of the day Jesus was presented to God in the temple, it also became a day when people celebrated the arrival of the light of the world - the son of God. He would then guide people to salvation and go on to die for their sins.

Candlemas Dates

Traditionally, Candlemas is celebrated on the 2nd of February, just like Imbolc. This day is also the 40th day of Christmas (Jesus's birth on December 25th), aligning with the Christian post-birth purification tradition. This is only the official festival, however.

Different churches tend to have different dates during which they celebrate the specific episode of the presentation of Jesus and not Candlemas as a whole. However, in the 5th century, the Roman Catholic Church was the first organized church to celebrate the episode during Candlemas on the 2nd of February.

Traditions

How Christians celebrate Candlemas can vary from one country to another and even from person to another. Like countries and churches, individuals create or add their own twists on traditions depending on the festival's meaning. This section, however, refers to the most common traditions observed by the Christian public.

Church

Most people go to church on this day to get into the spirit of Candlemas and connect with the meaning and intention behind it. The churches are often decorated with a near-infinite number of candles to celebrate the day.

Many people go to ask for purification or to dedicate themselves to God. Like it's common to consider New Year's Day as a day for new beginnings, many Christians take Candlemas as their day of new beginnings.

Candles

Another reason people go to churches is to either get candles that have already been blessed or get their candles blessed.

They then take their blessed candles home and light them throughout the year whenever they need divine help, hope, or guidance.

Traditionally, families also have feasts where they light candles to celebrate the arrival of Jesus at the temple.

Pancakes

While pancakes/crepes are mainly common in France and Belgium, they were a tradition adopted during the reign of the Roman Empire. At the time, Pope Gelasius I used to go down to the streets and pass galettes (savory crepe-like pastry) to the travelers who came to celebrate Candlemas in Rome, even though, at the time, it was not yet an official festival.

These galettes soon became a symbol of the festival. They were round and golden, representing the sun - the universe's main light source. Then, over the years, galettes were exchanged for the more famous crepes and became the traditional meal to have on the day of Candlemas.

Festivals and Processions

• Peru

The Virgin Mary has a lot of significance to many nations in South America. She first became known to them when the Spanish came to conquer Latin America. Gradually, the natives were converted to Christianity. That was when they were introduced to the maternal side of the Virgin Mary. To them, she was a protector of the oppressed, a source of strength for women, and a source of healing. This is why more than one country/city has adopted the Virgin Mary as a patron saint.

In Puno, Peru, the Virgin Mary is known as the Virgen de la Candelaria, which translates to the Virgin of Candles. While the main day of celebrating her is February 2nd, the Festival of Virgen de la Candelaria lasts for two whole weeks, from January 24th to February 13th.

It's one of Latin America's three largest festivals, next to Carnaval in Rio de Janeiro and El Día de Los Muertos (The Day of the Dead), a continent-wide festival.

• Puerto Rico

In Puerto Rico, the Virgin Mary is known as Nuestra Señora de Candelaria, which translates to Our Lady of the Light.

On Candlemas, the whole country celebrates her and the theme of light that is attached to the festival. A statue of the Virgin Mary is carried or driven through city streets all day. Then, the procession ends with the Holy Communion in a church.

Afterward, there are feasts, fireworks, dancing, and singing. People also light bonfires and candles to celebrate the Lady of the Light.

- Luxembourg

Just like Jesus, the child is the center of the story of his presentation at the temple. The children in Luxembourg are the main stars of Candlemas. They light candles and lanterns and walk down the streets in a tradition that resembles iconic parts of both Christmas and Halloween. They stop at each door to chant traditional songs, and, in return, they are given candy.

Candlemas and Imbolc

Having understood the three things that Candlemas stands for and its significance for Christians, we can now explore its relationship with Imbolc.

First of all, it's important to pinpoint the beginnings of the two festivals since it'll help you when considering one festival's potential influence on the other.

Pope Sergius I declared Candlemas an official festival in the 7th century. Nevertheless, historical evidence clearly shows that it had been celebrated for at least two centuries before that. Pope Gelasius I assumed the papacy in the year 492 A.D, and in his years, there was already a Candlemas procession.

Perhaps it was not official yet, but many have already celebrated the festival. And it was in those years that a Candlemas tradition of eating crepes developed.

Meanwhile, there isn't a specific date when Imbolc became a festival. Because the majority of literature on paganism and Irish mythology was either burnt, destroyed, or hidden during the Christianization of Ireland and England, resources are limited on the matter.

However, St. Brigid was born in the 5th century, and her name was based on Brigid, the Celtic goddess. This means that Brigid must have been known well before the 5th century, and if Brigid was known before that time, it must have been the same way with Imbolc.

So, the first piece of information is that Imbolc came before Candlemas in the 5th century, while Candlemas could have started before that. Now, this sort of vagueness can be frustrating, but there is one fact that could shed light on why the timings are close to each other.

Rome and Ireland were not Christian countries but pagan ones in the ancient past. They had temples, druids, altars, sacrificial grounds, and everything they needed to worship the gods. This went on up until the 4th century.

In 313 A.D., Emperor Constantine granted freedom from persecution to Christians. It started making its way to the top, and ten years later, it became the Roman Empire's official religion. When the tables turned, the Catholic Church and the Christian public started persecuting and forcefully converting unwilling pagans.

Pope Gregory I was one of the popes who led a diligent campaign dedicated to converting England and the rest of Europe. At first, he sent messengers, but they took too much time, so he ordered that the process be made faster through threats, violence, and the destruction of temples.

Then, one day in 597 A.D., he wrote a letter to the third Archbishop of Canterbury, Abbot Mellitus, telling him to stop the violence. "*Tell Augustine that he should by no means destroy the temples of the gods but rather the idols within those temples. Let him... place altars and relics of the saints in them.*"

He then says, "*[S]nice it has been their custom to slaughter oxen in sacrifice... Let them, therefore... on the feast of the martyrs whose relics are preserved in them, build themselves huts around their one-time temples and celebrate the occasion with religious feasting. They will sacrifice and eat the animals not anymore as an offering to the devil, but for the glory of God to whom, as the giver of all things, they will give thanks for having been satiated.*"

This speaks to a specific conversion technique employed by the church, which was to take something familiar to pagans and replace it with a Christian alternative. If this were done back then during the Christianization of Anglo-Saxon England and in Ireland starting from the 5th century, it could have taken place in post-313 A.D. Rome.

After all, it would explain the similar themes of purification, new beginnings, and the coming of the light. If the question were so easily solvable, it wouldn't have been a matter of debate for this long a time.

It's been long-debated because while the Christianization theory does explain certain similar themes, it indirectly nods to the very real possibility of Candlemas' independent existence.

After all, if Imbolc had truly been replaced, there must have been something to replace it. Perhaps the Christianization could have shaped some of Candlemas's traditions as the church hoped to create a more familiar environment for pagans. However, it's nearly impossible to say that Imbolc and Candlemas are different names for the same holiday or even different holidays until new data comes to light.

Candlemas, at its heart, is rooted in the Bible and the story of Jesus's presentation and Mary's purification. It's been a long-celebrated tradition since the Israelites were still making their way out of Egypt.

On the other hand, Imbolc is a celebration of the coming of spring, the end of winter, and the fertility and bounties associated with this time of year. Not just that, but it's also a celebration of the coming of Brigid with the summer months. It's also a long-celebrated pagan tradition with roots that go back to the time of myths which could go as far back as 4000 years B.C., if not further.

Either way, as we've said before, how you observe Imbolc or Candlemas is solely up to you. So, whatever your opinion of the two festivals is, the most important part of it is what it means to you. If you lose this personal and spiritual connection to the festival, it won't matter which belief or opinion you subscribe to.

Chapter 4: Flowers, Herbs, and Trees

Since Imbolc is the festival of the beginning of spring, many plants, herbs, flowers, and trees are associated with it. This chapter will go over all the plants associated with the festival and the goddess Brigid.

Some of these plants are known for being among the earliest signs of spring, and others are closely related to Brigid and Maman Brigitte. Meanwhile, others have an impact on one's energy and space, which can prove beneficial for pagans, witches, herbalists, and anyone else who celebrates the spiritual aspect of Imbolc.

As you read this chapter, you may be tempted to burn some herbs or work with some of these flowers. Of course, you should do what you feel called to do, but since we can't tell when this may be, here are the guidelines for working with any plant or herb:

- Always ground yourself before doing any spellwork. Because spells work on psychic, psychological, and physical levels, they need you to be in a focused frame of mind. In other words, you need to be centered and grounded, so you won't experience a sudden drop in your energy, physical pain, fatigue, or any other symptoms. This can be through meditation or any other technique - it's completely up to you. We will also expand on this in the spells and rituals section of the book.

- If you're going to use your herbs in a bath, you'll want to make sure they are clean before you allow them to contact your body.

- Always research the plant you are about to consume, apply it to your skin, or work with since some may be toxic or come with precautions.

- Make sure you are not allergic to the herbs and flowers you'll be using, especially their oils. The best thing to do is keep track of any symptoms, and with oils, you'll want to conduct a small test - which you'll find at the end of the chapter - before you use it.

With this being said, get ready to strengthen your connection with Imbolc as we explore its various plants, their symbolism, and how they're used to celebrate and honor the season and its goddess.

Flowers and Plants

Snowdrops

Snowdrops.

Snowdrops are one of the most famous plants associated with Imbolc. Think of it as the equivalent of Christmas and mistletoe.

The whole plant is small with a white flower. Out of the earth, the stem emerges, surrounded by two green leaves. Then, there's a white, drooping bell-shaped flower at the end of the stem.

It's the first flower to bloom at the end of winter, so it's so significant. Spotting snowdrops is one of the earliest signs that spring is on its way. It's a symbol of hope and a reminder that even the coldest and darkest days will end and give way to brighter and better ones. Last but not least, it's considered a sign of Brigid's return.

Coltsfoot

Coltsfoot.
https://pixabay.com/images/id-1274956/

Coltsfoot is another flower commonly associated with Imbolc and Brigid. Like snowdrops, they too bloom in the early spring. Their flowers are a stunning yellow, similar to dandelions in shape.

Coltsfoot is associated with Brigid, and its corresponding planet is Venus which, like Brigid, also has a heavy association with the divine feminine. This is why Coltsfoot, too, is known for its use in spells related to love, healing, and wealth. It's a great flower to burn during divination, as well.

Overall, if you want to work with Coltsfoot, Imbolc is the time since it's during their season and the season of their goddess.

Be careful when working with Coltsfoot because it contains a group of alkaloids (to defend itself against predators) that have been shown to cause liver damage. You can only become affected if you consume the flower.

Blackberry

Blackberries are very closely associated with Brigid for more than one reason. They are Brigid's sacred fruit, and because they fall under the planetary influence of Venus, blackberries represent everything that has to do with the divine feminine.

Just like Brigid and Venus are associated with healing, love, and prosperity, so are blackberries. Primarily, however, during Imbolc, blackberries are used for their healing and rejuvenating properties. Whether they are put in baked goods, eaten by themselves, or used in spells, blackberries can be quite potent when used at this time.

Chamomile

Chamomile is a popular and effective ingredient used in many spells and rituals. It's associated with the element of water - one of Brigid's elements - and is known for its ability to purify and protect. Not just that, but it's also associated with many sun gods.

With the coming of spring, it's important to purify one's space and energy as one embraces the arrival of the sun and the Earth's revival. Purification can put you in the right headspace to accept what the spring has for you. It can also bring you a sense of peace and balance due to its properties relating to the water element.

The best part is that Chamomile is a very versatile flower. It can be brewed into a tea, put in a bath, burnt, steeped in water, sprayed for protection against spirits, candle magic, etc.

Tansy

Tansy.
https://www.pexels.com/photo/a-close-up-shot-of-tansy-flowers-6891103/

The word Tansy is derived from the Greek word *athanatos* which means immortality. It's all because the flower does not die easily and can survive various temperatures. They die late in the winter, letting their seeds fall into the ground, only to be born again.

They are a symbol of rebirth and the fact that death only makes way for a new birth. This makes it a true parallel of the cycle of life and the season change from winter to spring. In addition to its connection with Imbolc, the flower can be associated with Brigid, who is known to represent rebirth and renewal.

Tansies are mainly used in longevity spells. Tansy flowers and oil are sometimes used to honor the bodies of the deceased. Last but not least, they are added to dairy-based baked goods to celebrate Imbolc.

What's crucial for you is that eating Tansies can harm you. They are toxic in large amounts, and as little as ten drops of the oil can cause death. So, make sure you abide exactly by the recipe.

Lavender

Lavender is a calming herb with cleansing, healing, and calming properties, especially when combined with other herbs. It's the perfect herb if you are determined to get in the right frame of mind for Imbolc.

You can burn it, brew a tea out of it, or use it in baths to take away the negative energy from yourself or your space and calm yourself down. It is a great way to ground yourself and practice self-care on this day, especially if you've had a tough winter. And, if you feel called to work with Brigid, you can always prepare a cup of lavender tea for yourself and another for the goddess.

If you consume too much lavender, you may have to deal with a few minor side effects such as constipation, diarrhea, and headaches.

Daffodils

Daffodils bloom late in the winter or very early in the spring, making them one of the most closely-related flowers to Imbolc. Their bright white and yellow colors are also a strong reminder of the coming of light.

Looking at, growing, and meditating on daffodils can help you connect with the bright spirit of Imbolc. It will help you get in tune with nature and its patterns. Not just that, but they're also one of the perfect plants to add to your altar if you want to channel that essence of Imbolc.

Celandine

Celandine, specifically Greater Celandine, is a little bright yellow flower associated with the sun and the element of fire. Needless to say, it's also closely tied to Imbolc and Brigid.

The name is derived from the Greek khelidōn, which translates to the bird species, the swallow. In Ireland, the swallows arrive in the spring (April). Celandines get their name because they start to bloom a little while before the swallows migrate back to Ireland.

The flower is known for its protective properties, especially in legal matters. Nevertheless, it's also known for its powerful toxins if consumed raw - even in moderate amounts. When using it, herbalists make sure to calculate an exact dosage, so if you use it, make sure you always get the dosage right or follow the exact recipe.

Iris

Irises are beautiful flowers known for their large petals, delicate but showy. They are the birth flowers of those born in February, which makes them one of the main symbols of Imbolc.

The meaning of the Greek word iris is rainbow. This speaks to the symbols attached to the flower, like hope and the coming of spring. Not just that, but Iris was also the name of one Greek messenger of the gods. She was the link between the physical and spiritual worlds.

That is why it was common to find purple irises planted over graves, especially those of women. It was an offering for the goddess to help the dead navigate their new environment. The same flowers were also taken to symbolize Maman Brigitte and her identity as a death spirit.

While Irises can smell heavenly, they can also be toxic because they contain the compound iridin, which can cause nausea, diarrhea, pain, and vomiting when ingested. Some Irises can irritate your skin when their leaves or roots are touched.

Violets

Like purple irises, violets are also considered one of Maman Brigitte's favorite offerings. They are also known as February's birth flowers, especially because they bloom during the late winter and early spring. They are a reminder that Imbolc is the time to bloom or start blooming.

As for their uses and associated meanings, the flower's beauty makes it a perfect ingredient for love and fortune spells. Meanwhile, the flowers can be great protectors as their beauty overwhelms and scares away malicious spirits.

Last but not least, there are many ways to consume violets. They can be eaten alone, sautéed, or steamed. They can be put into soups, herbal teas, and baked goods. You can even glaze them with sugar and eat them candied.

Herbs

Bay Leaves

One little-known fact about the silvery leaves of the fascinating bay leaf is that you can use it for cleansing just as you would use sage and palo santo. This makes them a perfect way to welcome Imbolc.

As powerful and potent as they are, they are also gentle leaves that can be written on and burnt to release or manifest. Primarily they are associated with growth, cleansing, and healing.

They can be used with salt to cleanse a house or in a bath to cleanse one's energy. They can also be used to attract abundance, wealth, and good fortune.

Heather

Heather is known as a plant that stands for growth. It's ruled by Venus and the element of water, which is why it reflects certain aspects of Brigid, mainly rebirth, new beginnings, beauty, and peace.

It's a powerful herb to be used when preparing for Imbolc, especially because this is the time to begin anew and start planning ahead. Heather also attracts positive energy and can provide protection.

Finally, it's one of the best ways to bless a new couple, a new relationship, or a new endeavor.

Rosemary

Rosemary is a very powerful herb, one of the most powerful, in fact. Its association with Imbolc comes from its cleansing and protective properties. Given that Imbolc is the time to shed whatever is old and harmful to make way for the new, it's a perfect time to use Rosemary.

You can burn it alone or in a bundle to cleanse your space and magical belongings (wands, tools, etc.). Rosemary oil is great for cleansing objects, as well. As for the raw herb, you hang it somewhere for protection or use it to make decorative wreaths that you can charge with intention.

Angelica

Angelica

https://www.pexels.com/photo/delicate-angelica-archangelica-with-small-leaflets-5349219/

The Angelica flower's Latin name is Angelica Archangelica. It's a flower deeply associated with angels and archangels. Needless to say, anything like that would be a great source of protection in preparation for any endeavors you want to attempt during the spring.

While the leaves can break spells and hexes and be put in protection bags with other herbs to keep you safe, the roots and stem are also quite magical. Tea can be made from the roots. You can also put them in your shoes to make sure you attract the people and energy for which you're looking. Lastly, the stems can easily be turned into a flute.

Basil

Basil is a beautiful herb that packs quite a punch behind it. It's used for protection. Some people argue it can draw out scorpion venom. Meanwhile, others associate it with evil, so they believe you must curse the ground it grows in for the plant to grow properly.

To protect yourself, you can put basil in your house. You can also keep a leaf or two in a prosperity bag to attract wealth. The sweet and enchanting smell of basil is also why it's a great choice for love spells.

Vanilla

Vanilla is a plant deeply connected to Venus and elemental water. It has a sweet, calming, and pacifying effect that provides a sort of healing warmth. This makes vanilla incense a great choice to have around during Imbolc. After all, it's when internal warmth is just as needed as external warmth.

If you work with spells or feel drawn to them, you'll get the best results from vanilla when you use it for fortune, love (even self-love), sex/desire-related rituals, and spells.

Ginger

Have you ever eaten ginger and felt a burn? Just like you feel this physical burn, you should also feel a metaphysical burn as ginger helps ignite one's internal fire. Given that the element of fire rule it, this makes the use of ginger very fitting during Imbolc.

Ginger's fiery nature makes it very effective in achieving spiritual and mental clarity by purifying and healing. If you're in a relationship or are looking for one (or even a fling), putting ginger in a spell bag for attraction will heat things between you and your crush or your significant other(s).

Thyme

Thyme is one plant that has been widely known and used by various cultures throughout the ages, from ancient Egyptians to the Greeks. It's been used in embalming bodies, purifying, cleansing spaces, and even incense.

If you're planning on doing some self-healing during winter's last days, thyme is an herb you'll want by your side. When you're about to take on new tasks and need prosperity and good fortune, thyme is the way to go, too. Also, it's one of the best herbs to use if you want to clear out negative emotional energy, perhaps after a fight, a rant, or after releasing pent-up emotions.

Trees

Oak

Ages ago, the oak was a sacred tree to druids. They provided a sense of security and protection. Because they often lived for centuries and had a maximum lifespan of 500 years, they were also a symbol of wisdom and strength, not to mention that people depended on their wood in nearly every aspect to survive, from houses to weapons.

Because the oak is masculine and feminine, it is a great tree to work with if you are trying to connect to either of your aspects. More importantly, it's a great tree to have at your altar or to have your altar made of, especially if you want the aid of what the oak represents as you approach the spring.

Rowan

Rowan is a sacred Celtic tree deeply associated with the tree of life, and it's a symbol of protection and wisdom. In the Celtic tree calendar, it's the one associated with February. People used to plant a rowan in front of their house to protect them in the past. Others used a simple sprig.

The rowan tree is also associated with the maiden aspect of the triple Goddess, which corresponds to Brigid. So, whether you want to celebrate Imbolc, honor Brigid, or appreciate the delicate solemn nature and powerful influence of rowan trees, make sure to set aside time to work with tree sprigs or even plant new seeds.

Willow

The willow is closely associated with the divine feminine and the sun, among other planets. It is associated with sensitivity, intuition, emotions, and introspection. At the same time, it is associated with the maiden aspect of the triple goddess.

It's a beautiful reminder that even though winter is hard, it is not a time to escape but be taken advantage of. The tree also presents an invitation for you to work with it and reflect upon your previous winter so you can learn your lessons before beginning the summer seasons. The willow also invites you to connect your divine femininity with the coming of spring.

Resins

Myrrh

Myrrh is a gum-resin extracted from a type of tree called Commiphora myrrha. It's one of the staples for rituals, spells, and veneration of gods and goddesses. Some people link it to the element of fire, but its healing properties make it more of a water-type.

The resin is used in protection and banishing spells which are two things many of us need, as they cut ties with what doesn't serve them, be it toxic relationships, a malicious spirit or person, or something else. In ancient Egypt, the resin was also used when asking Isis for help or working with her.

Having read this list of plants, their connection to Imbolc and Brigid, and how they can serve you during this time, there is one thing you should keep in mind. The list, truly, is endless. These are the most popular plants, and the ones we feel help us celebrate and connect to the spirit of Imbolc.

Your practices, beliefs, and what you feel drawn to on your spiritual journey should guide you when selecting or experimenting with herbs and flowers. This chapter was only a roadmap and a list of suggestions. All the decisions are completely up to you.

Oil Allergy Test

Before experimenting with the plants and their oils, it's important to conduct this simple allergy test to avoid any mishaps or grave consequences.

1. Dilute the oil by adding a few drops of essential oil to twice the amount of water.
2. Wash your arm with unscented soap for sensitive skin.
3. Add a few drops of the diluted mixture to a small area of your skin.
4. Place a bandage over that area to prevent the oil from getting washed away. Keep it on for a day. If you notice any symptoms, like itchiness, redness, etc., then take off the bandage, rinse the area immediately, and stay away from that oil. You can also place a few drops on a band-aid and apply that for a quicker alternative to the bandage test.
5. If your skin doesn't react in 24 hours, you're free to enjoy all that your oil of choice offers.

Chapter 5: Crafts and Decorations

Decorations are not put up just so your house can look better. It does feel that way sometimes, but it really isn't. It's the equivalent of dressing up for a special occasion. You know that you're about to go out to celebrate something, you feel happy, and you're in a good mood. Perhaps you want to take some pictures to remember the event, too. So, to express all of this, you dress nicely.

Making crafts and decorations for Imbolc is a form of self-expression. When you're celebrating a season or a milestone in the year cycle that is/has become so important to you, it's natural to want this happiness and excitement to reflect on your space. After all, our space reflects who we are and what we value.

More importantly, it's a way of connecting to Imbolc on a very deep level. When you're making crafts, you're not just making objects. You're making things similar to those made by ancient pagans hundreds of years ago. These things bear deep meaning and beautiful emotional and spiritual significance – and they are/have been used in rituals that not only honor Imbolc but the goddess Brigid.

Making crafts and decorations can be really fun, especially if you have kids. Fun is important on Imbolc. Perhaps some of us can get carried away with the mental and spiritual side of Imbolc, and others can feel like they are being called to do something else. Of course, we all celebrate in different ways, but don't forget that we are celebrating the coming of spring at the end of the day.

While it is easy to lose oneself in the serious aspects, remember that fun is an intrinsic part of Imbolc. It's a festival that should be joyously celebrated. So, take the time to reflect on your winter, plan for your spring, and purify your space, but also allow yourself to have fun and get excited about spring and the coming of Brigid. Then, allow this excitement to show in the form of decorations.

This chapter is all about creating crafts and decorations from scratch. We will talk about the most popular decorations of the occasion, their connection to Imbolc, and what exactly is done with these objects.

St. Brigid's Cross

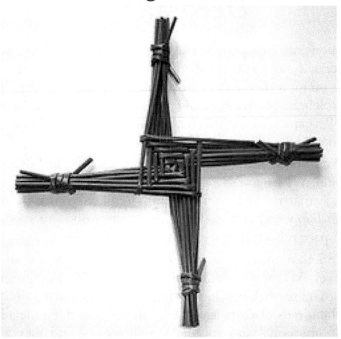

Saint Brigid's Cross.
Culnacreann, CC BY 3.0 <https://creativecommons.org/licenses/by/3.0>, via Wikimedia Commons: https://commons.wikimedia.org/wiki/File:Saint_Brigid%27s_cross.jpg

St. Brigid's cross, also known as the Celtic sun wheel, is one of the most famous Imbolc decorations. Not only that, but it is a form of adoration and a way to honor Brigid. After all, this cross is her symbol, and it represents the sun, of which Brigid is a goddess.

The symbol may look like a cross, but it is a set of spokes that connect at the center. These spokes reference the sun wheel, the solar disc, or the wheel of fire which all connect to Brigid.

Before Imbolc, these crosses are made to honor Brigid and her return. After the winter months, the goddess brings the sun with her to spread warmth on the earth. So, in celebration of this act, we make these crosses to remind ourselves of the goddess's blessings and celebrate the spring's return.

The cross can also be your way of asking for the goddess's protection and blessings on your home and loved ones. It's up to you, your relationship with Brigid, and the intentions you set.

Materials

- 17 12-inch reeds, pipe cleaners, straw, or rushes. You can use one of these materials for the cross. It's completely up to you to choose, although we recommend a natural material rather than an artificial one.

  The number of reeds you use will determine the size of your cross, so it's also completely customizable. If there is a number that represents something to you or that you particularly connect to, it's a great idea to use it.

- Four pieces of string - these will only be used to tie the arms of the cross at the end, so you can substitute the pieces of string with more reeds or rushes if you know how to tie them.

Spiritual Preparation

- The St. Brigid's cross ritual started on the 1st of February at midnight in the distant past. When the reeds were gathered, the people would welcome Brigid as they brought the reeds into the house. Of course, now we understand that the gods and goddesses care about what's in our hearts more than what we do. So, if you'd like to, you can welcome Brigid in your own way as you bring the reeds into the house (during your preferred time of the day).

- After you've gathered your materials, cleanse them in warm water (if you can) and clean your space. If you are a Wiccan, feel free to cast a circle to outline your sacred space - or not if you feel like you don't need one.

- Take a little bit of time to ground yourself, then gradually shift your focus to Brigid. Because this cross is an act of love for the goddess, you'll want to put intention into your creation. So, before you start, take a few minutes to set your intentions and focus on your relationship with Brigid.

Instructions

1. Take one reed and hold it horizontally with your thumb and index finger. This will be the main reed - the spine - and we will place all the rest around it. One of your hands will be used to keep the reeds tight around the center.

2. Take another reed with your other hand, fold it in half over the main reed to create the letter "T," and keep it tightly in place with your thumb and index finger. The fold should be facing you, and the separate ends should be facing the ground.

3. Make a 90-degree turn (anti-clockwise) so that the main reed is vertical and the second reed is pointing to your right.

4. Grab another reed and fold it over the second reed. It should be parallel to the main reed, and the loose ends should be pointing downwards.

5. Make another 90-degree turn and fold another reed over the main reed in the same way as before. Make sure it's tight around the center.

6. Then, make a 90-degree turn to complete the circle and fold another reed over the last one you placed.

7. Repeat this process until you get the size you want or until you're down to your last reed - you'll need one reed to secure the rest of the reeds in place before you tie them.

8. Once you've done this with your reeds, don't let go. Make sure to keep them held tight; otherwise, they will go all over the place.

9. With the last reed, the process will go a bit differently. Instead of folding the reed in half, wrapping it around the cross's arm, and keeping the ends loose, trap the ends inside the folded reed. The last reed should make a 90-degree angle with the folded reed it's trapped in.

10. Make sure all the reeds are tight around the center, then bundle together the ends that make up each arm of the cross.

11. Tie each arm with a piece of string or with a long reed.

Uses

Brigid's cross doesn't only have to be used during Imbolc. There are many uses for this beautiful symbol. In addition to its being a celebration of Brigid and a source of protection and blessings, you can place it on your altar or in a space to keep Brigid's presence near you. You can also burn it as an offering to the goddess.

After Imbolc

Because St. Brigid's cross is a sacred symbol and one that may absorb negative or malicious energy to protect you, you must dispose of it correctly. At the end of the year (next Imbolc), or if you're permanently leaving your space, you must burn the cross and bury its ashes in the earth as an offering.

Don't forget to express your gratitude to the cross and Brigid.

The Brigid Doll

The Brigid doll is a symbol of Brigid, the maiden. Imbolc is also a celebration of Brigid's rebirth and the transformation from crone to the maiden, so this doll represents this new beginning.

It's a way to invite the maiden's fertility, abundance, potential, life force, confidence, and curiosity into your house. Not just that, but it's also a way of observing and celebrating these qualities in the goddess herself.

In the early days, the Brigid doll was made using woven wheat or oats to celebrate the earth's fertility. Although, these materials may be hard to find now. If you can find them, by all means, go ahead and get some. However, if you can't, there are other options, like straw and corn husks.

Materials

- Corn husks or Straw - a few hours before you start, put your straw in warm water and let it soak to make it bendable.
- Yarn
- Cotton balls (only for corn husk dolls)

Spiritual Preparation

- Take some time to relax your thoughts, become calm, and set your intentions for making the doll. Since it is a celebration of Brigid's maiden aspect, that's what we recommend you focus or meditate on before starting. However, what you focus on is still your decision, so trust in yourself.

Instructions

Corn Husk Dolls

1. To make the head, you'll need to take a husk, fold it in half, and put in a few cotton balls, ideally two. It depends on how big you want the head to be.

2. After putting the balls in, lift the husk around them, and apply a little pressure right above to trap the cotton balls and twist the husk. Then, take a piece of yarn and tie a tight knot to create the head. Make sure you leave a length of husk from the front and back to make the torso.

3. Take two husks, fold them in half - or as much as you need - and tie a knot half a centimeter (less than half an inch) away from each end. The husks should form the arms, and the small, spread-out parts should form the hands.

4. Tuck the arm/hand husks into the torso husk, twist to trap the arms and tie a knot to form the waist.

5. To form the skirt, put two slightly overlapping husks on a dry surface, place your doll on them, and place another two husks on top (also slightly overlapping. Make sure you align the tops of the husks with the doll's waist.)

6. Press the tops of the husks together around the waist and tie a tight knot to connect the skirt to the waist.

7. Gently pull the doll's skirt down from its face and arrange it how you'd like it to look. You can also take a pair of scissors to the skirt and even it out, or even give it a distinctive design.

Straw Dolls

1. Take many straws (10 -15) and tie them together about half an inch from the end. This will make up the head's length, width, and size, so you can customize the number of straws and where you place your knot from the straws' end. We recommend you try it out first as it helps you to understand how it works.

2. One by one, bend the straws upwards at the knot, folding each straw into itself.

3. Flip the straws upside down and tie another knot around the bundle that forms at the top. You've just created the head and the body.

4. Take half the number of straws you used for the head and tie a knot down their middle to create the arms.

5. Part the body straws evenly and place the arm straws in-between. Make sure you hide the middle knot with the straws that make up the body.

6. Slide the arm straws to the height you'd like. Ideally, you want it to be close to the head knot to stabilize the arms. After you're satisfied, tie a knot under the arms to keep them in place.

7. Tie two knots, one on each arm just a little ways from the end, to create the hands. If you don't like the length of the arms, tie the knots wherever you'd like on the arm, then cut the extra straw with a pair of scissors. Make sure you leave a small bit of straw to create a noticeable hand.

8. To create the bottom half, spread out the leftover length of body straws, then trim the excess to create a proportionate bottom. For a better-looking doll, make sure your knots are very tight.

9. An optional step is to color your doll or decorate it with herbs.

After Imbolc

Like with St. Brigid's cross, if you ever want to or need to dispose of your Brigid doll, burn it in a fire and present its ashes to the ground.

Brigid's Bed

If you're planning to make a Brigid doll, then there's nothing better than Brigid's bed to go with it.

On Imbolc, Brigid comes to visit her people and bestow upon them her blessings. Just as a Brigid doll is a symbol of the goddess, the bed is a welcoming gesture, and it's something that Brigid truly appreciates.

Brigid's bed is a miniature resting place for the Brigid doll. Once you make the bed, place the doll in it and either place it by the fire - if you have one- or in your kitchen next to the cooker/oven.

Materials

- Wicker basket
- A receiving blanket, a small bed sheet, or any type of soft cloth
- A small blanket

Spiritual Preparation

- If you're planning to go through this much effort to receive Brigid into your home, she must be one of two things; a beloved old friend or a new friend you're looking forward to meeting. Keep your mind on how Brigid would react upon seeing the bed you're making for her. This will help you keep your intentions focused on this act of love.

Instructions

1. Line your wicker basket with a receiving blanket or any other type of soft, delicate material to serve as a bedsheet.
2. If you have a miniature pillow, put it in there. If you don't, you can make one by sewing together two pieces of cloth around some cotton or any soft and fluffy material.
3. Fold a small blanket and keep it at one end of the wicker basket for Imbolc night.

Uses

If you want to invite Brigid into your home as you're having Imbolc dinner, place your doll in the bed with the blanket over her and a candle, or a few, next to her - make sure you observe fire safety precautions.

Some people prefer to make a ritual out of it and put the Brigid doll in the bed as they sleep at night.

Regardless of what you choose to do, Brigid will see your intentions and efforts, and she will bless you and your household.

Ice Candles

Ice candle

Ice candles are a fascinating creation. More than that, they are a perfect symbol of what happens on Imbolc. The sun starts approaching, gradually melting winter's ice, and banishing its cold.

Materials

- A double boiler or a pot and a steel bowl - you can substitute the bowl for a pan, but it wouldn't be as ideal.
- Paraffin wax or chunks of used candles
- A large, empty milk carton
- Wick
- Mold sealer
- Small chunks of ice
- Colored dye (optional)

Ratios: The ratio in this recipe is equal parts ice and wax. The amounts depend on the size of your container. For example, if you'll be using a quarter of a 32-ounce milk carton, then you'll need four ounces of each.

Spiritual Preparation

- If you'd like to set any intentions while making your candle, you can either do that before you make the candle or when it's done. Both are good options, but they are different. We recommend you channel your energy and intentions or ask a deity to bless your candle before you make it. This makes the experience rather personal and uniquely intimate.

Instructions

1. To make the candle mold, cut the top off the milk carton leaving only the size of your desired candle.
2. Make a very small hole with a pin or a needle at the bottom of the carton. Make sure it's right in the center.
3. Slip the wick into the hole and gently drag it out from the other side until there's an extra inch of wick extending from the top of the carton.
4. Coil what's left of the wick at the bottom of the carton, press it against the carton and cover it with a mold sealer to make sure the wax and ice don't leak out.
5. Turn the carton so that it's sitting on its bottom. Place a pencil or a chopstick across its edges, then coil and tie the extra wick around this pencil while ensuring it's taut. This

is important since it'll guarantee a straight wick.

6. After that, it's time to prepare the candle. Cut your paraffin wax or old candle wax into small blocks using a knife, a hammer, a chisel, or a screwdriver.

7. Fill up about a quarter of a pot and place the metal bowl or smaller pot/pan inside it. You don't want the water to touch the surface of the second pot. As you heat the water to a boil, the steam will heat the pot and melt the wax.

8. Pour the wax chunks into the double boiler, then when the wax melts, that's when you can add the dye to color your candle. If you use old candles, you'll already have an interesting mix of colors.

9. When the wax is ready, take your ice out of the freezer and arrange it inside the carton. Make sure it's snug around the wick, and make sure that the wick is centered. Then, pour in the wax. Ideally, you'll want to place a large container lined with aluminum foil under the carton to control the damage in case of any leaks or accidents.

10. Ice candles usually take about an hour and a half or two to cool down completely. Leave yours to cool before you peel off the carton. And make sure you peel the carton over a sink to avoid spilling any remaining water.

11. Completely trim the bottom wick.

12. Trim the top wick to a quarter of an inch.

13. Leave the candle to dry completely before using it, and then place it in a shallow bowl or another container to catch the molten wax and enjoy!

Uses

- The beauty of an ice candle is that it can represent more than one thing. It can represent the coming of spring. It can represent Brigid's return. It can even represent you or your life. Perhaps this winter has been a hard one, or perhaps you suffer from a seasonal affective disorder that drains you. The candle can symbolize your fire that will soon burn bright.

- You can also use the candle on your altar or when you're meditating.

- The candle could be a perfect accompaniment to the Brigid doll and Brigid's bed as it can represent the goddess's dual elements: fire and water.

Chapter 6: Setting Up an Imbolc Altar

Imbolc ritual altar.

As important as they are, altars are not for all pagans or practitioners. How we interact with the gods and nature depends on how we prefer to interact. Many of us consider altars a safe and sacred space where they worship, pray, and more. Meanwhile, other theist pagans simply don't feel the same way. Some don't worship deities (non-theistic pagans), so they don't have a pressing need for an altar. Last but not least, some pagans tend to steer clear because altars can be triggering for them.

This is all to say that the importance of an altar is not an objective one but a very subjective one. If you're new to paganism, you deserve to form your opinion on altars. You'll want to read through this chapter as we will discuss altars in general before delving into Imbolc altars.

On the other hand, if you have already figured out your stance concerning altars, this chapter will serve you greatly, or it will just be an interesting read and nothing more.

In this chapter, we will discuss how to keep an Imbolc altar or decorate your existing altar for Imbolc and everything that has to do with altars.

Altars

An altar is a sacred space for you to worship in any way you please. In our modern world, they are not just for pagans and Wiccans but also used by organized religions. However, this doesn't mean that they belong to one and not the other. The concept of an altar is a neutral one that you can give whatever meaning you like.

Imagine a "secret spot" where you usually go to meet a friend or to be alone and think for a little while. This spot is comfortable and has a few of the things that you like around it. And, when you go there, you experience a feeling of calm almost instantly, or you can't help but remember your companion who often goes there with you. An altar is exactly like that.

It's a place for you to nourish your spirit and tend to your spiritual needs. It's also a place for you to worship your deities of choice, connect with them, and ask for help. More importantly, it's a physical manifestation of your deities' spiritual presence, which can put a smile on your face whenever you look at it, better yet, help you when times get tough.

When it comes to witches and Wiccans, altars serve another purpose besides the rest. They are a sacred and safe space charged with energy and intentions where the person can perform spells and practice their craft.

What the Altar Should Look Like

There isn't really one standard altar set-up even though, in the past, there was a traditional approach to Wiccan altars.

The more humanity has grown in understanding, the more we've come to grips with the fact that the look of one's altar should depend on what one wants to do with it.

If you want to worship deities, it makes sense to include some of their symbols, perhaps a picture, a symbol of their element, plant, and anything else you may want.

If your ancestors are the ones you'd like to ask for guidance, then you may want to place some of the objects that deeply connect you to your family upon your altar.

If you intend to connect with the universe and its energy, you'll want to have a few natural items - crystals, seashells, feathers, herbs, flowers, etc.

If you'd like to keep your altar a workspace so you can practice witchcraft, it makes more sense to go easy on the symbols and keep more of your frequently used ingredients and tools, like candles, Tarot cards, mortar, and pestle, etc. On your altar.

If you'd like to celebrate a particular occasion or an event, like Imbolc, you can create a new set-up (or exchange your existing one) that resembles how you feel about the event.

So, as you see, an altar's look is not fixed. It can change to suit your purposes and intentions, what you're currently drawn to, or what you need.

As for how cluttered/fancy your altar should be, we'll tell you the same thing we said since the beginning of the chapter. It's up to you and the resources at your disposal. At the end of the day, what an altar looks like is nothing compared to what it means and the power it holds.

Keeping Your Altar

Your altar reflects your spiritual side, and this is why we keep recommending that you follow your instinct. Whatever you are drawn to will shape your altar, and as you grow and build a connection to your special space, it will change to reflect this growth and connection.

Here is an outline and a loose guide to help you create your own altar, as we've done before. We'll leave the customization to you.

The Purpose of Your Altar

The purpose of an altar will determine how you proceed with the next steps, which include finding a location, building, decorating, cleaning, and so on.

We've already tackled the various purposes of an altar, from worship to witchcraft, but finding your own purpose can be a bit challenging.

Some of you may have that purpose clear in your head. Others may feel strongly drawn to building an altar, and that's it. Now, there are two approaches to finding the purpose of your altar. One is to narrow down your choices, and the other is to embrace the infinite possibilities.

To narrow down your choices:

Consider how you feel when you get the urge, though, or call to make one.

Do you feel a sense of excitement or safety? If so, what makes you feel that way? Some people feel excitement at the thought of getting to explore their relationship with certain deities. Others feel like they yearn for the safety and warmth of a space they can dedicate to their complex range of spiritual needs.

In addition to exploring your feelings, it's always helpful to explore your imagination. What do you see yourself doing at the altar? Are you meditating? Burning incense? Talking to some spirit or deity? Grounding yourself? Asking for help? Perhaps you imagine doing all of these or none of them.

To embrace the unknown:

The purpose of your altar could be to explore your spiritual aspects. Some people like to know what they're going to do on a trip. Others like traveling without an itinerary because it leaves room for them to do what they truly feel like doing.

Because your altar is yours and only yours, it can be that safe place that allows you to explore what feels right for you. Embracing the possibilities means creating this blank canvas, paying attention to the colors you're attracted to, and listening to what your soul, heart, mind, and body feel like painting.

If this seems a little vague now, don't worry. You'll understand more with each paragraph.

The Location of Your Altar

An altar is sacred, and so are the items on it. So, the ground rules are:

- Don't put it somewhere where it's easy to bump into it.
- Don't put it somewhere where it may be desecrated.

Now, these may be rules, but they are also things that simply make sense.

You wouldn't put a new crystal vase in your cat's favorite place to bask in the sun. It would get knocked down in less than a day.

If you get a new chair knowing that your dog often has "accidents" because he doesn't believe in peeing outside, wouldn't you take the necessary extra precautions?

That said, let's talk about where you should put your altar.

Location is about safety. In each of our homes, there is always that place we're attracted to the most. It's a place we feel comfortable. It's also a place where we can sit all day, especially with a nice drink or something after a hard day. This is the type of place you want for your altar.

This place could be somewhere in your bedroom, your living room, by a window, in the attic, or in your favorite corner/nook. In the far distant past, people used to keep their altars in the kitchen. Even now, kitchen altars have their own unique signature that differentiates them from other altars.

Because the kitchen resembles the heart of the house - it's where food is cooked and where the fire is constantly burning - it was always considered a great place to set up an altar. Nowadays, a kitchen is not just that, but it's also where we get to touch, smell, listen to, taste, and feel nature's many elements.

A kitchen altar can serve as a reminder that there is worship even in life's most routine and mundane aspects. It can bless and protect your kitchen and the meals you prepare. Moreover, it can help you further connect with nature, its magic, and the magic of combining different ingredients and creating a whole new thing. Finally, it's a great way to celebrate Imbolc for many reasons that we will delve into later in the chapter.

Unfortunately, some of us don't have the luxury of publicly practicing our beliefs, so your favorite spot in your bedroom will do just fine. You can even use a small or foldable surface as an altar, and that way, you can store it and take it out whenever you want to.

The Building Process

An altar consists of two main things, a surface and sacred items. Some people choose to put a tablecloth over their altar's surface for decoration, to protect the surface, or because the color or design of the cloth means something to them. However, it's not at all necessary. In fact, it can be a nuisance if you'll constantly need to clean it from melted wax.

Another group also considers an offering plate as essential, and it is, but only for them since offerings are a big part of their worship.

So, the rule of thumb when it comes to your altar is that if you don't want it, then you don't have to have it.

Now, without further ado, let's explore the two main components of an altar.

• The Surface

This could be a surface you have in the house, like a counter, a coffee table, the top of a microwave, a shelf, or even a lazy Susan. It could also be a make-shift surface, like a wooden box, a cardboard box, a crate, a shoebox, etc. As long as it will be able to carry your items, it'll be perfect.

This is where your items will go, and if you are using the altar for practical purposes, it'll be where you work. That means that based on the purpose of your altar - or what you think it is - you'll have to decide how much space you need. This may sound like a crucial point, but it isn't. The worst-case scenario is that your altar will be a bit cramped, and that's okay, as long as you're comfortable with it.

- **The Sacred Items**

Now that you've got yourself a surface, all you need are a few sacred items, and you'll be good to go.

This is the most fun part about creating an altar for many because imagination is your limit. As long as you feel connected to the items you put on it, you're doing it right. So, what sort of items are we talking about here?

People who design their altars to reflect their love for nature and the universe like to include one item to represent each of the four elements:

- **Earth**: A stone or a crystal
- **Fire:** Candle
- **Water:** Shells, sea glass, sand dollars, sea/ocean water (or any kind of water)
- **Air:** Feathers, bird-shaped pins/statues/trinkets, incense

Nature-oriented pagans also like to include plants like sunflowers, lavender, roses, violets, etc. A plant is also a great choice if you plan to work with a deity who a particular plant symbolizes. You can place a dried leaf, a small branch, or a twig onto your altar.

Speaking of deities, pagans who work with and/or connect to specific gods decorate their altars with pictures or statues of the gods or of animals that represent them. For example, if they worship Odin or the Morrigan, they'll put a crow to symbolize them.

They may also add plants or symbols associated with the gods onto their altar. For instance, if they worship Brigid, they'll put Brigid's cross or a piece of oak.

Some people choose to put one or two items from their childhood. Perhaps, a special item connects them to an ancestor or one they always saw magic in. It could also be an item that provided them with a sense of safety when they were children.

Then some often use their altar to speak to their ancestors and ask for help and guidance. These people add pictures of their deceased loved ones and perhaps some items which belonged to them.

The list of items you have to choose from is endless, which can put a little pressure on you. Remember that it's okay to expand your altar, have more than one, or even replace one item with another. And as for the placement, it's completely up to you.

Remember, what you choose to put on your altar shouldn't have to abide by others' standards, and it shouldn't have to be "cool," "eclectic," or "eccentric." All it needs to be is something that you feel will be appropriate. More importantly, remember that your altar's magic and power come from within you and not from the objects.

The Cleansing Process

Cleansing is an important part of keeping an altar. Just like anything else, the items on the altar can absorb negative energy, especially if you put them there with that intention. At some point in time, the environment around your altar will become saturated with this negative energy.

There are many reasons to cleanse your altar:

- When you feel that the energy has become too negative.
- The first time you make an altar.
- When you bring a new item or use a new surface.
- When you change the purpose of an altar, like when you're celebrating Imbolc.

There are also many ways to cleanse your altar. The two most popular ways are:

- You can burn sage or myrrh and let the smoke absorb the energy. Make sure that you leave a window open so the smoke will have a chance to leave the house.
- You can spray seawater or holy water (water and salt that has been blessed in the way you feel is right for you) or water left under a full moon for a night.

Imbolc Altars

Imbolc altars are not much different from normal altars. The only difference is the sacred items you put on it, which are purely determined by your relationship with Imbolc. With Imbolc altars, you'll find that you can be more detailed with what you put on them since celebrating Imbolc is a very specific purpose.

When decorating your altar for Imbolc, apply everything you've learned so far in this chapter to choose a location, a surface, and your sacred items.

Altar Preparation

If you already have an altar, you don't have to make a new one. You can cleanse it, remove the items that don't fit with your way of celebration, adding those ways that do.

On the other hand, if you don't have an altar, you can have the Imbolc altar as your first or set up a kitchen altar if you'd like to. Don't forget to choose a place that reminds you of life, rebirth, the coming of spring, or Brigid. You don't have to change your altar's location, but it may add a different flavor.

As for kitchen altars, all you need is a lazy Susan or a tray as a surface and your choice of sacred items. Because the kitchen is Brigid's domain - it's the heart of the house and where the fire is - it's a perfect place to set up an altar for her. And, because Imbolc is when plants and animals come to life, you can include nature-related sacred items to celebrate spring and the fruitfulness that comes with it. It'll serve as a beautiful reminder of how connected to nature you are - what you're cooking came from the earth, which is made fertile by the sun's return, which is what you're celebrating.

Imbolc-Related Sacred Items

There are two main types of objects you can add to your Imbolc altar. Depending on your beliefs and what you feel comfortable with, you can choose these items.

Brigid-Related Items

These are the items that symbolize Brigid or that are associated with her.

- Brigid's cross
- Bull statue, picture, etc.
- A piece of oak bark
- A statue, a painting, or a drawing of Brigid.
- A crescent (The first phase of a new moon, which represents the maiden aspect of Brigid.)
- Candles, especially red, white, and green
- Red or orange crystals/stones, like amethyst, sunstone, and peridot
- Snowdrops
- An offering plate

Nature-Related Items

Imbolc, after all, is a celebration of the return of spring which makes it a celebration of nature.

- Plants, like daffodils, snowdrops, Irises, and rowan trees.
- Animal statues, specifically cows and sheep.
- Candles
- Incense
- Crystals/stones
- Tarot cards (It could be a way to set intentions for the spring.)
- Runes
- A miniature bonfire

After Imbolc

After Imbolc, all you have to do is figure out what you want to keep and what you want to throw away. Whatever you'd like to keep, cleanse it, and keep it in a safe and clean place. Then, cleanse your altar like you'd cleanse a new altar and put your day-to-day items.

Now, disposal of offerings, sacred items, and altars is one issue that plagues almost everyone who keeps an altar. Setting up an altar for a one-day occasion seems like a whole impossible ordeal.

Because everyone deserves to celebrate Imbolc without worrying about the day after, here is your comprehensive disposal guide.

Organic or Degradable Objects

When it comes to anything degradable, it's okay to burn the object and bury it in the ground. Before that, however, make sure that it won't harm the earth, soil, or plants. Suppose it will; maybe *compost it* instead of burning it.

Inorganic or Non-Degradable Objects

When it comes to anything that won't decompose on its own or that will pollute the atmosphere if burnt or buried, it's best to cleanse the item however you see fit and then find a different way to dispose of it.

You can give it away or swap it with someone if it's a statue. If it's a used candle, you can melt it with a little extra wax (or more used candles) to make new candles. If it's a recyclable object, recycle it. Always remember to cleanse your items before you dispose of them, though. You don't want to pass on anything unwanted to anyone unaware.

Offerings

Different traditions have different tips on how to dispose of an offering. First of all, there is no specific waiting period that you must leave an offering for so that the gods can eat it. For the gods, it's all about the intentions and the essence.

Second, there are many ways to dispose of an offering. As long as yours is respectful and environment-friendly, you can do what you want:

- You can eat the offering.
- You can burn it and then present it to the ground.
- You can throw your offering into a body of water.
- You can feed it to an animal.
- You can compost it.

Chapter 7: Recipes for an Imbolc Feast

One of the beautiful things about Imbolc is that it's one of the very food-orientated Sabbats. Since spring is the time when most foods grow, animals reproduce, and milk production flows, Imbolc has long been associated with the coming of not just the season but with everything it has to offer.

This abundance of food-inspired ancient pagans to create recipes based on what was most popular with the coming of spring to celebrate the land. Nowadays, we still celebrate this tradition, even though the recipes may have changed a little - or a lot.

Imbolc Recipes vs. Regular Recipes

What separates a regular recipe from an Imbolc recipe are the ingredients used and the blessings and intentions added. Neither cuisine nor cooking method nor dietary restrictions can make your meal less "Imbolc."

The coming of spring celebrates an increase in milk production, which means that an Imbolc recipe should include milk and/or other dairy products. It also celebrates the time chickens start laying eggs, which makes eggs a part of the celebration. Third, it's a celebration of the Earth becoming fertile again, which opens the door to oats, potatoes, wheat, vegetables, and the flowers and herbs we mentioned earlier in the book.

As you read through the recipes, you'll notice that there are some ingredients more common than others. It's also why the cooking style isn't the be-all and end-all - and the ingredients, too, if we're being honest. Granted, the ingredients have some significance, especially for people who love tradition, but it's a celebration of nature at heart. As long as nature is involved, you're on the right track.

As for the cuisine, our recipes are mainly Celtic because Imbolc was primarily celebrated among Celtic cultures. However, keep in mind that paganism did not represent and is not strictly tied to Celtic cultures. Imbolc is a celebration of nature, making it a festival for all peoples and cultures. This means there's always room for you to celebrate with the cuisine you like most.

Things might have been different if you were honoring Brigid or preparing an offering for her on this day, though. In this case, it makes more sense to prepare Irish or Celtic recipes since Brigid is an Irish goddess. Even then, an offering is more about what the food holds and represents rather than the food itself, so many would argue that it still won't matter what cuisine you cook.

Well, what if you can't cook at all? Well, that's no problem. This chapter has a selection of easy recipes that are guaranteed to become firm favorites for you and the people you celebrate with.

Side Dishes

Rosemary Potato Rolls

This vegetarian recipe is a great Imbolc dish if you're a fan of herbs and if you want a little extra cleansing and protection. To get ready for the spring, rosemary can help you start fresh. As for the potatoes, they're a classic Imbolc food, just like the butter and milk in the recipe, which are also a celebration of Brigid.

Ingredients
Yield: 14 rolls

- 3 oz. (approx. 90 ml) or ⅓ cup and ½ tbsp. butter
- ¼ cup sugar
- ½ tsp salt
- ½ cup milk
- An egg
- ½ cup mashed potatoes
- 2 & ½ cups all-purpose flour
- 1 tbsp. finely chopped rosemary

For the yeast mixture:

- 1 & ⅛ tsp or 4 grams of yeast
- ¼ cup warm water

Preparations

- Boil and mash the potatoes.
- Beat the egg.

Instructions

1. Heat your milk until it starts to bubble, then set it aside.
2. While the milk heats, add the yeast to the warm water and stir carefully to ensure the yeast is properly distributed in the water. You should see foam in the cup within five minutes. If you don't see foam, try with a new pack of yeast.
3. Mix the sugar, salt, and butter in a mixing bowl, then add the milk when the mixture gets too lumpy.

4. Gradually pour half a cup of flour into the mixture as you stir.

5. Add the egg into the mixing bowl along with the yeast mixture.

6. Mix in the potatoes and the rosemary.

7. The dough should be in a more liquid form than a solid one, so stir until it's completely smooth before adding what's left of the flour, then keep mixing.

8. Sprinkle a little flour, just enough to cover your work surface, before transferring the dough from the bowl. You want to prevent the dough from sticking, but you don't want to use too much flour that dries it out.

9. Knead the dough until there are no more lumps. As you knead, pay attention to your dough. If it's too sticky, add more flour. If it keeps crumbling, use a teaspoon to add more milk.

10. Use oil or butter to lightly coat the inside of a bowl, then put the dough into it, cover it with a cloth, and leave it for 45 minutes to rise in your oven or microwave - or any warm place.

11. After the dough has risen, lightly coat a cupcake or muffin tin with oil, then pinch off medium-sized chunks from the dough, ball them up, and place two to four balls in each slot.

12. Cover the tin (or tins) with clean cloths and leave it in a warm place to rise again for about 30 more minutes.

13. At the 20-minute mark, preheat your oven to 375 F or 190C.

14. Bake the rolls for 15 minutes or until you can insert a toothpick in the middle of a roll, and it comes out clean.

Possible Variations

- The best thing about herbs is that you can put them in anything. Because this is a sort of sweet bread, you can add lavender, vanilla, or violets.

- For more savory bread, you can decrease the sugar (to taste) and add a sprinkle of pepper, then add your choice of herbs. Thyme, basil, and bay leaves are great additions.

- If you don't have the time to make mashed potatoes, you can use instant mashed potatoes instead.

Savory Dishes

Colcannon

Colcannon is a traditional Irish salad-like dish made of potatoes and kale or cabbage. It's an Imbolc dish that showcases potatoes and celebrates spring's effect on the soil.

Ingredients

Yields: 5 servings

Because this dish doesn't depend on the ratios of its ingredients, you can get as creative as you want with the amounts.

- 2 russet potatoes
- Half a bunch of kale
- 3 spring onions
- Ice
- Salt
- Pepper
- 1/2 cup or 4 oz. unsalted butter

Preparations

- Peel and quarter the potatoes.
- Chop your onions - you can add texture to your dish by varying your chopping styles.

Instructions

1. Bring a pot of water to a boil, then let it simmer.
2. Add a dash of salt, put in the potatoes, and let them cook until they are soft in the middle. A knife should be able to slip easily through the potato.
3. While the potatoes cook, bring another pot of water to a boil, then throw in your kale. Let it flash-cook for a minute, then take it out and put it in a bowl of ice-cold water.
4. When the kale's temperature goes down, leave it to drain.
5. In a blender, throw in 2 chopped spring onions (⅔ of the entire amount) and add the kale. If you want texture, pulse for a few seconds until everything is roughly mixed. If you

want a smooth kale-onion mix, work the blender for a little more, or use a food processor.

6. Go back to the potatoes. Drain them, but keep them in the pot if they're done.

7. Add butter to the potatoes and mash with a masher, a spatula, or even using the bottom of a mug.

8. Add the kale and onion mixture to the potatoes and any other spices you might want.

9. Season with salt and pepper, and enjoy.

Possible Variations

- This recipe is great because it leaves so much room for creativity. You can add your own herbs, vegetables, and even spices. If there's something you feel like you need to try, go ahead and chuck it in there. We recommend you try basil, rosemary, and thyme.

- Cheese is a great addition to this recipe, whether it's added when you're mashing the potatoes or as a topping. Ideally, go with a salty cheese to balance out the butter.

- You can add a little protein to your dish by frying bacon or cooking minced meat or chicken. Simply toss it in when you have mixed all the ingredients.

Cheese Pasta

This is a simple dish that most of us can cook in our sleep. It also happens to be a modern Imbolc dish. The ancient Irish didn't necessarily depend on mac and cheese in their daily lives, but cheese on its own was almost a necessity. Even better, cheese, among other dairy products, is an Imbolc food. And what's pasta made of? Wheat that comes from our fertile earth.

Ingredients

Yields: 7/8 servings

- A 1 lb. (500g) bag of pasta (any shape)

- 4 cups (1 quart) of cream

- 8 ounces or ½ a pound (250g) of goat cheese

- 2 tbsp rosemary

- 1 clove garlic
- Salt
- Pepper

Preparations

- Crush and peel the garlic
- Chop the rosemary
- Chop the goat cheese into cubes.

Instructions

1. Bring a pot of water to a boil, add 1 tablespoon of salt (or 1 and a ½), then throw in the pasta. Let it cook until it's al dente - until it's mostly soft but still has that bite to it. Then, drain the pasta.

2. Over medium-low heat, pour the cream into a large saucepan, then add your rosemary and the clove. You can also add any other spices.

3. Let the cream simmer by keeping the heat medium-low until you notice little bubbles on the surface. You don't want a full-blown boil because then the cream may curdle.

4. When the cream thickens, add the goat cheese cubes, and stir.

5. Gradually, the goat cheese will start to melt, and you'll have your sauce.

6. Salt and pepper to taste, then add your sauce to the pasta in the pot or vice versa. Then, mix well and enjoy.

Possible Variations

- This recipe is a vegetarian one, but you can add cooked chicken to the sauce before combining it with the pasta.
- Once again, you can add as many herbs as you want depending on what you like or the benefits you need.

Desserts

Lemon Almond Cake

This recipe is butter-free which is great since most Imbolc foods tend to rely heavily on dairy. However, that's not the best thing about it. The light-yellow color of this cake is a beautiful reminder of the sun. Not just that, but the almond flour also serves as a nice nod to Imbolc since almond trees start blooming during this time. As for the lemons, they provide a beautiful, refreshing flavor that, unlike other desserts, won't make you want to keel over and slip into a food coma.

Ingredients

Yields: 7/8 Servings

- 1 1/2 cup (144g) finely ground blanched (without almond peels) almond flour

- 1 tsp baking powder

- 1/2 cup (100g) white sugar

- 4 large eggs separated into whites and yolks (see how below)

- Zest from two medium or large lemons

- 1/4 tsp ground cardamom

- 1 tsp white vinegar

- A pinch of salt

- Powdered sugar

Preparations

- Over a small bowl, crack an egg, but hold it vertically as you separate the shell to keep the yolk from falling. Then, gently pour the yolk into the empty half of the shell. Repeat a few times until all the egg white is in the bowl. Transport the yolk into a separate bowl and repeat with the other three eggs.

- Preheat the oven to 350 F or 170 C and grease a pan of your choice, preferably an 8-inch mold, with oil or butter.

Instructions

1. Put your yellow ingredients - the yolk and the lemon zest - into a bowl and a quarter cup of sugar. Whisk or mix until smooth.

2. Then, it's time to mix your dry ingredients. In a separate bowl, add the flour, cardamom, baking powder, and any other dry ingredients you'd like to add - vanilla powder, instant coffee, etc.

3. Add your dry ingredients to the egg yolk mixture and whisk until they're one thick, uniform mixture. It should look a little crumbly, like wet sand.

4. You can use a manual whisk for this step, but it would be much easier to use an electric one. Start beating the egg whites slowly at first, then work up to a faster speed. Once you see bubbles, add a pinch of salt and vinegar to help your egg whites turn quickly into a fluffy cloud-like mixture. Add the sugar. Once the mixture turns into this cloud-like texture, add the rest of the sugar and mix. Only stop when the mixture is strong enough to form peaks when you lift up the whisk.

5. Gradually add the meringue (egg white mixture) dollop by dollop into the cake mixture. Fold every dollop of meringue added to the mixture until there's nothing left. Don't whisk because you don't want the fluffy meringue deflating.

6. Pour/scoop your batter into the mold, level it, and bake for 30 minutes - or until you can stick a toothpick through the center and it comes out clean.

7. Let the cake cool before you slice it.

8. Top with powdered sugar, lemon curd, or lemon whipped cream.

Possible Variations

- You can turn this recipe into a cupcake recipe by baking at 400 F or 200 C for less time.

- Lavender can be a great addition to this recipe, especially if you'd like to offer a slice for Brigid.

How to Imbue Your Food with Magic

There are two good ways to give your food an extra magical kick.

Focusing Intentions

We always hear about food being made with love, but no one ever takes it seriously. It's just something we say. What if it isn't just that? What if there's a little more meaning to the phrase? Because there is.

Love is a force. It's a vibration. It's transferable. You can send it to other people, and, in the same way, you can also send it to objects.

The simplest way to imbue food with happiness, gratitude, warmth, love, etc., is by focusing on your intentions and channeling your energy into the food.

You simply need to ground yourself (through meditation, breathing exercises, or any of your preferred methods), then channel your energy into your ingredients before you start working.

When you're working, try to stay connected with this energy. The easiest way to do that is through music. You can play love songs, happy songs that make you feel safe and calm, etc.

After you're done, do the same with the end product as you did with the individual ingredients- you don't have to touch it; hovering your hands above it is enough.

Sigils

Sigils are a simple and effective way to imbue food with magic, and they cover a much wider range of attributes than transferable intentions because they can embody magical intentions. You can have sigils for protection, prosperity, growth, peace, happiness, etc.

You need to draw your sigil of choice on your food with a toothpick.

There are two ways to go about sigils. You can use pre-existing sigils and runes based on your own beliefs, or you can make your own sigils, and here's how:

First, you've got to ground yourself. Take a few moments to find your center and calm yourself.

Then, when you're ready, start shifting your focus toward your intention. What effect would you want your food to have on those who eat it? What do you want to give them? When you find the right words, say them out loud.

The key here is to say them as facts. In other words, speak from a place of trust in the power of your sigil. For example, "This cake brings abundance to those who eat it,' instead of "I hope this cake brings them abundance."

If the words feel right, grab a pen and a paper, and write them down. You can write a full sentence as in the past example or just the magical intention, abundance.

Ultimately, sigils are symbols. So, you need to create a symbol from the letters of the sentence or the keyword. You can use all or only a few. It doesn't matter as long as it feels right to you. Remember that this part is purely creative, so there is no right or wrong.

Once you've created your sigil, it's time to conduct an activation ritual.

Go to your altar. If you don't have an altar, just create a safe spiritual atmosphere somewhere in your house - you can light up a candle and burn some herbs or sage.

Sit in front of your sigil and speak your full intention out loud, just like you did before. Repeat your intention a few times - if there's a number that bears significance to you, have it be your number of repetitions. By doing this, you are affirming the sigil's purpose.

Once you've finished, fold the four corners of the paper inwards and seal the paper with wax - preferably sealing wax, but regular wax works as well. This part is parallel to the symbolic sealing of the sigil's meaning.

After this step, place the folded paper on your altar.

Your sigil is now ready to be used, so feel free to draw it on your food, skin, air, or wherever you want.

Chapter 8: Imbolc Family and Group Activities

A huge part of Imbolc is the community with which you celebrate. Now, this doesn't mean that those who prefer to celebrate alone or have no choice in the matter should miss out on the essence of the festival.

Celebrating alone is different from celebrating with a family or a group. Alone, you can introspect and delve as deep as you want into your thoughts and emotions. You can also worship in a way you feel comfortable. You get a fully customizable experience and, if you choose to, a rather deep one. You also get to cook your own foods and spend one-on-one time with nature and your deities.

On the other hand, with a group or a family, you get to share the experience with other people who have a similar special relationship with nature. As one, you get to be together, celebrating the coming of spring and/or Brigid.

Perhaps you won't have as deep an experience, but you'll have a broad one. You'll get to listen and witness how other people celebrate Imbolc, and if you have children, then you'll get to see them spiritually growing. Overall, you'll feel an overwhelming warmth and a sense of togetherness.

We recommend that, for Imbolc, you separate your day into two parts; one for celebrating alone and one for celebrating with your community. And, because we've spoken about solitary festivities significantly more than group ones, we will flip the scales in this chapter.

Throughout this chapter, you'll get to read about many group activities, not just for adults but for children too. You can feel free to do them as they are, add your twist, or use them as a building block to build your own unique traditions.

Spring Cleaning

Spring cleaning is a very popular tradition in many parts of the world, especially in the U.S. Without knowing its origins, you may have thought that the event is a tad too random. After all, why spring? What happens during that time that makes it customary to do some deep cleaning?

Well, each culture has its own reasons. For pagans, however, we choose to clean on Imbolc because it's our new beginning. Like death gives way to life, winter gives way to spring, and we consider that return of light our new beginning.

As the light returns, as life starts to bloom once more, and as we come to life after a season of low activity and demotivation, we start cleaning our houses and cleansing our bodies. It's a way of saying, out with the old and in with the new.

Spring cleaning for Imbolc can be fun, especially if you have kids. You can try so many ideas that won't make it feel anything like a chore.

Make a Playlist

Whether you want to make an Imbolc playlist or a spring-cleaning playlist, all you need to do is add a bunch of songs on the days leading up to Imbolc and crank up the volume on the day.

You can even use Spotify to create a collaborative playlist, share the link and have every member of your family/group contribute with their own picks. Your playlist will have something for everyone, from "Here Comes the Sun" by The Beatles to "Irreplaceable" by Beyoncé.

Raise the Stakes

The best defense is a good offense. You've got to raise the stakes if you want to take spring cleaning for Imbolc to a whole new level.

We suggest you make a game plan, assign each person a role, a room, or a domain, and then pick out rewards for the best performance.

You could add points for creativity, points for taking no prisoners - as opposed to hoarding, and points for thoroughness. The criteria are up to you but don't forget to make the reward worth it.

If you enjoy it, this could become an annual family tradition - your own version of the Olympics.

Clean with Purpose

There's a difference between cleaning as a reaction to a dirty house and cleaning with a set purpose. Of course, when Imbolc cleaning, the purpose is to declutter your space and let go of what you don't use anymore. It's also to make space for what is yet to come to you that year.

Taking a little time to connect with that purpose can do you wonders. You can have your family or group sit in a circle and then go around saying what you want to get from this year's spring cleaning.

Lighting a Fire

We've already spoken about the significance of fire during Imbolc, so we'll talk about how you can light one safely and what to do in a gathering around the fire.

Campfire

If you have a wood burner or a fireplace, chances are you already know how to use it. In this case, you don't have to light a campfire. However, if you do have access to the open space and would like to be with nature on this day, then a campfire is exactly what you want.

You'll Need:

- A level piece of dirt-covered ground
- Rocks
- Tinder - small twigs and dried leaves
- Kindling - slightly larger twigs and thin branches
- Firewood

- A matchbox or a lighter
- Water

Find a dry, dirt/sand-covered ground or a flat rock. If you can't find an area like this, you can clear out a patch of grass - although we don't recommend that for obvious reasons. The point is that you can't light a fire on a flammable object, so you need dirt or rocks.

Then, place medium or large rocks in a circle to create your fire ring and gather some tinder in the middle.

Over the tinder, place two pieces of kindling in a crisscross shape. You can also place eight pieces of kindling, two to each side, in the shape of a square.

Light up your tinder and tend to the fire, adding more tinder until it's big enough to burn the kindling. Blow on the base of the fire to make it burn stronger.

When the fire is strong enough, add in your firewood.

Last, and most importantly, don't leave your fire unattended. Always keep it under control, and keep some water - or a small fire extinguisher - next to you at all times.

Fire-Oriented Activities

- **Fire Manifestation**

This is a simple ritual you can have with your group where you write your goals and wishes on bay leaves, then throw them into the fire.

You can either go round the circle, share your wishes out loud, or keep them to yourself and connect to the energy and focus that come with group settings.

- **A Reflective Sit-Down**

Fire is a great element to meditate on and to be used for divination. It can help you get into a trance state, and it can help start conversations among people. This makes it the perfect time to reflect on your past year, share your thoughts and anxieties about the future, and share what you love about Imbolc. There are also dozens of Imbolc prompts online that can help start a dialogue between you and your family or community.

Organizing a Feast

Who doesn't like food, especially when it's with the people you love and celebrating a festival that you love? Also, food is also a way to bond with other people. You can exchange recipes, learn techniques, and eat food inspired by different cultures and imaginations.

Now, you can prepare all the food and take care of everything feast-related, but that can be a little too much effort. Instead, you can prepare a menu with your family and have everyone come up with a dish or a course and prepare it. Especially if you have kids, this can be a great idea. Don't leave your younger kids alone in the kitchen, though. You can also have a dish party where every group member gets to bring in a dish.

Imbolc Cooking Challenge

You already know a few ingredients that we consider Imbolc essentials. Instead of having an ordinary dish party, you can turn the heat up. You have two options to do that - both are great fun.

With each option, you'll need a few pieces of paper (as many as the participants) and a pen. For the first challenge, you're going to write the name of an Imbolc-related herb or flower on each piece of paper. Carefully fold the pieces of paper enough so that no one can see what's written inside. Then, mix up the papers and let each person draw a piece of paper.

People will have to prepare their dishes while ensuring that they include that one ingredient on their piece of paper.

The second challenge goes the same exact way except that, instead of an herb, you'll put a list of ingredients on each paper, and these must all be included in the dish.

Group Divination Ritual

Divination is also a great group activity to practice with your people. Not to mention, Brigid is a goddess associated with divination, especially fire divination. Plus, rather than practice it alone, your people will help you get in the zone. You can all help each other focus while, at the same time, doing this act of love for each other. Overall, it will help you get closer and get in tune with each other's life journeys.

Fire Scrying

A bonfire is perfect if you want to go into a trance-like state. So, if you'd like to, you can practice fire scrying, but only if that's a form of divination you're comfortable with practicing. An advantage of fire divination is that you can light a fire and plan your entire evening around it.

Tarot Cards & Runes

There are also Tarot cards and runes, both of which can engage the whole group and help strengthen the bonds between its members. This sense of community is very important, especially in a world where practicing paganism can get a little lonely.

Stream of Consciousness Writing

Another method that can work for people who don't practice divination or scrying is a stream of consciousness writing. It's where you take a piece of paper and start writing out your thoughts. They don't have to make sense. They only have to be your authentic thoughts.

It's a psychological technique that's supposed to help you be mindful of the thoughts going on in your head and your senses. Nevertheless, it can also help you get through to your deepest thoughts, inner child, and higher self.

At the end of the day, it's not about the technique itself; it's about the quietness and the active awareness that the exercise provides. It creates an environment of openness that will allow you to listen to or access the area you want to access inside you.

Bardic Circle

A bardic circle is essentially an artists' get-together. In the past, bardic circles were where bards used to sit together in a circle, often around a fire, and live performances and recite poems. It was a celebration of the imagination, creativity, and the arts. It was also a celebration of Brigid, the muse of all poets and the goddess of inspiration, wisdom, and poetry.

In your own bardic circle, you can have it as a purely artistic gathering, or you can also include Brigid. Remember that you don't have to honor Brigid if she's not a goddess you work with or if you don't feel comfortable.

If your people are already in touch with their artistic side, you can have them each bring one of their works (or create a new one) to show the group and speak about it for a bit. You can also ask your group to bring their instruments and tools for impromptu performances.

Last, you can propose a particular theme or a natural element to make your bardic circle more interesting. A common element will bring out each person's genius and unique perspective. As people start seeing how they look at the same thing, they'll begin appreciating their creative side even more.

On the other hand, if your people aren't really in touch with their bardic side, you can pass out papers and pens - you can also use your phones - then give out a prompt.

This prompt could be a complete sentence, like "And as life coursed through nature and plants rose from the ground, one didn't." It could also be an incomplete sentence, "Mother Nature caressed her cheek and smiled, then said..." There are also dozens of online poem/story prompts.

Inspired by these prompts, your people should start writing their short stories or poems. Give them a good five minutes, then ask everyone to stop. Afterward, let them read out their creations. You don't have to worry about things like grammar and structure. This is only a creative writing exercise that's supposed to engage one's imagination and help people connect over their stories.

Before you start a bardic circle, you must create a safe space for your people to share their art. It may help if you agree on a few ground rules before you begin or if you go around stating intentions before you begin. Remember that you can't expect someone to share openly if they don't feel safe enough to do so.

Planting Seeds

What's more festive than planting new seeds? When celebrating this joyful coming of spring and the signs of new growth in nature, it's only fitting to grow your own trees or plants.

The best part is that you don't need any special tools or requirements. You can plant trees in your community garden, in the forest, in the backyard, or in your coven's garden if you have one.

If you have kids, or if your kids are new to Imbolc, this activity will be more than perfect because it will help them tune in to nature and its cycles. It will also help them understand what Imbolc is about.

There are many seeds to choose from, so we'll classify them into fast-growing and slow-growing - all of which can be planted on Imbolc.

Fast-Growing Seeds

- Spinach (winter varieties)
- Lettuce
- Sunflowers
- Basil
- Cilantro

Slow-Growing Seeds

- Cactus
- Coneflowers
- Sage

If there's a plant you feel particularly attracted to, don't hesitate to research it and see if you can plant it in February. By all means, don't feel limited to this list.

After deciding on a seed to plant, you can practice adding intentions to the seed. And, as your plant grows, don't forget to talk to it and give it love, whether through touch or kind words. According to a study done by Deepika Choube and Shubham Sharma, positive and negative words directly impact a plant's growth.

Candle-Making

For starters, candle making is a fun activity that will help you get rid of your used candles and get you a cool new one.

Candle making is also a great activity that resembles rebirth. Over the year, you use up your candles until they're no more. Then, during Imbolc, you experience your own return of the light as you turn your spent candles into one whole candle.

Now, what makes group candle-making great in particular is the end product.

If you melt your own candles, you'll probably have an idea of what colors you'll end up with. However, when you melt candles with a group, there's no limit to the colors involved. There's also no way to predict the end result.

Imagine if five people put all their year's used candles into the mix. That's at least five colors, assuming they're not avid white candle fans.

As for the process, it's almost identical to making ice candles. The only difference is that you skip out on the ice here.

Ask your friends to cut their wax into small chunks and bring it with them.

Then, you can either have people choose their colors and melt the wax accordingly or just pour everything into the double boiler and mix well.

You can add colored dye if you want to introduce a whole new color. You can draw a sigil to imbue the candle with magic. Or, you can add fragrance oil to make the extra candle special.

You can also use mason jars or reuse old jars as containers for your candles. You have to clean the jar and let it dry while you make the wax. Then, attach the wick to the bottom of the jar by dipping it in hot wax and quickly pinning it to the bottom of the jar. The wick should hold steady as long as you don't pull on it aggressively.

Keep your wick straight using the pencil method as you pour the wax into the containers and leave them to dry.

Meanwhile, you can sit with your friends and eat, talk, or do any of the activities we mentioned above. For example, you can even make a classy event out of the whole evening, candles, and lavender wine. And, at the end of the day, everyone gets to go home with a new treat for their altar or house.

Chapter 9: Spells, Rituals, and Baths

In some of the past chapters, we've discussed how to celebrate Imbolc on a physical level. We've talked about the most popular Imbolc foods and the crafts and decorations. Even when we spoke about altars, we didn't delve deep enough into the spiritual side of Imbolc festivities. In this chapter, however, we will go as deep as we can into the spells, rituals, and spiritual baths that can be done during Imbolc.

Now, Imbolc is one of the best times to cast your spells and practice divination, especially if you channel the element of fire into your practices. Brigid's association with healing and magic, combined with her powerful return during Imbolc, can give your spells a special kick.

Main Themes

At Imbolc, we try to focus on spells and rituals that have to do with the main themes of this event. The whole of nature - and the universal energy - goes through the cycle that comes with the seasons. This is why certain spells will naturally be more effective than others if their purpose and intention happen to be in sync with the natural cycle.

Throughout the book, we've discussed Imbolc's main themes:

- Rebirth
- The coming of light
- New growth
- The end of winter/darkness
- Abundance
- Fertility
- The return of fire

These are the themes we'll draw inspiration from in this chapter, and they're also the themes that you can build your spells on.

Keep in mind that each theme bears influence on so many of life's aspects that there's a near-infinite number of magical intentions you can extract:

- New opportunities
- Banishment
- Attraction
- Release
- Cleansing
- Healing
- Rejuvenation
- Motivation
- Fertility
- Fortune
- Abundance
- Focus
- Motivation

These are only a few, and we'll try to provide you with spells and rituals for as many intentions as we can. For the rest, we'll provide you with an all-purpose spell that you can customize depending on what you need.

Spells

All-Purpose Candle Spell

This spell is a great choice if you're still a beginner or if you have too specific an intention that you'd like to realize. Given the use of candles, it's a very fitting choice for Imbolc, especially if you like or are interested in working with Brigid. Fair warning - the spell can be a little time-consuming.

Ingredients

- A taper candle - can either be a plain white candle or a colored one. If you associate a certain color with a particular intention or a question, you can use that. If you don't want to, that's fine. It's completely up to you.

- Pen or a small blade

- A match or a lighter

- The moon (optional)

Instructions

1. Start at nighttime. Prepare your ingredients, cleanse your space, and set the mood, so to speak.

2. Ground yourself. This spell takes a lot of focus and concentration, and it requires you to be mindful of your intentions. It always helps to be calm when doing this sort of spell.

3. Figure out your intention and make it known. You can do this by speaking it out loud and repeating it a few times. Then, hold your candle in your hands and channel this intention into the candle.

4. Take your pen or small blade and write/engrave the thing you wish to attract or banish on the candle. For attraction purposes, to attract wisdom, for example, write the name of the thing from top to bottom. To banish something, like pain or jealousy, write the name from the bottom up.

5. Place the candle in front of you and light it. As it burns, focus on your intention, and envision it coming true. Try to remain focused for as long as you can.

6. When you feel like you've spent enough time or when you start losing your focus beyond return, blow out the candle.

7. Give gratitude to the candle and the universe and any deities you've asked for help (if any), then burn what's left of the candle and throw it away. If you've used soy wax, coconut wax, or beeswax, you can bury the candle in the ground. Paraffin wax, on the other hand, can be harmful to the soil.

Additional Information

- If you feel a special connection with the moon and would like to include it in your spell, time your spell with the phases of the moon. A new moon will help you attract what you want. A waning moon will help you get rid of what you don't want.

Abundance Spell

This spell is a beautiful source of abundance, especially if you need something quickly. It works great for job/career opportunities and decisions that are out of your control. Keep in mind that this is a candle spell, so make sure you're safe.

Ingredients

- Enough gold candles to form a circle (about eight)
- A picture where you're smiling
- A medium-sized mirror
- Lighter or matches

Instructions

1. As with all candle magic spells, start yours at night too. Choose a place where you can prop up your mirror later while doing the spell, then cleanse that space.

2. Sit by yourself, find your center, and connect with your intention.

3. Arrange your candles in a circle and make sure they're stable enough so that they don't fall.

4. Place a smiling picture of yourself in the circle's center.

5. Start lighting up the candles slowly. Light one at a time in a clockwise direction and speak from your heart. You can chant a verse you've composed about the return of the light and the igniting of your own fire. It can rhyme, but it doesn't have to. You can also say what you specifically want. It doesn't matter what you say as much as your intentions.

6. Repeat your words or channel intentions while lighting each candle.

7. Stabilize the mirror against a wall or a surface to see the whole circle. Then, ask for twice the fortune or twice the abundance.

8. Sit with the candles for as long as you can maintain your focus. Then give gratitude and, ideally, let the candles burn out. Blow them out if you're not comfortable leaving the candles overnight or until they burn out.

9. When the candles are out, clean your mirror while chanting everything you chanted the night before. Then, pick out a place where the sun enters your house and prop the mirror so that it can reflect the morning light.

10. Every time you pass the mirror, stop and look into it and say, "I will thrive with the abundance I am given," or anything with the same meaning.

Rituals

Starting a ritual
https://unsplash.com/photos/x5hyhMBjR3M

When it comes to rituals, the guidelines are much looser than spells since they're all about you and your psychology, spirituality, and psychospiritual. Meanwhile, spells involve working with energies, deities, and different types of magic.

As you read through these rituals, feel free to customize them.

Fertility Ritual - Brigid's Cross, Doll, and Bed

The Brigid doll represents the goddess, and it carries her blessings, most of all, fertility. The bed is a gesture and a symbol of welcoming the goddess, and therefore her blessings, into your house. As for the cross, it's a celebration of Brigid's power, and it serves as an offering for Brigid and a request for her protection.

Combined together, these three objects can be of great power, whether you decide to put them on your altar, near your fireplace, or in the kitchen.

All you have to do is:

- Put your intentions into making the three objects, and don't hesitate to ask Brigid out loud what you want while doing so.

- On the eve of Imbolc, before you go to bed, put the doll in her bed and ask Brigid one more time to bless you or your household with her fertility.

- As an offering, you can leave a cup of milk for the goddess.

- You can also leave the cross as an offering or hang it somewhere in your house to receive Brigid's protection. Of course, you can also make two crosses and do both.

Thought Seeds Ritual

Imbolc is a great time to start harnessing your drive, planning your way and acting on your thoughts, turning them into habits. This ritual embodies the spirit of Imbolc and the new growth it brings into people's lives. It should be mentioned that this ritual includes keeping a plant alive. If you can't do that, it's recommended that you stick to our modified version.

Growing new seeds is a real-life parallel of how our thoughts can turn to helpful habits that finally bloom/bear fruit. In this ritual, you'll charge a few seeds with intentions, and, as a result, their growth will reflect on your life.

Requirements

- Your choice of seeds
- Empty plant pots
- Soil mix (suitable for your seeds)
- Pen
- Bay leaves

Instructions

1. Write what you'd like to grow within yourself on the bay leaves - one thing for each leaf. Keep your intentions focused as you write, and make sure to keep your language growth-oriented and not oriented towards dispelling.

2. Fill less than half of each pot with soil, then focus your intentions on more time and give the bay leaves your gratitude as you place one in each pot.

3. Fill up the rest of the pot and plant your seed.

4.Water the seed, tend to it, and care for it. As you do and as you care for yourself too, you'll start seeing the plants growing with your intentions and feeding your drive more and more.

Modified Version

The modified version of this ritual focuses on the psychological aspects of the ritual instead of anything else. So, here, you'll simply plant the seeds without including the bay leaves.

What makes this a ritual is that it will mark the starting point of your journey. As you plant the seed, picture the thought seeds you planted in your own head, whether by working on yourself, healing, or practicing a new skill - it could be something personal, relational, or professional.

Tending to the plant will remind you to tend to yourself as the days go by. More importantly, noting the small signs of growth in your plant will help you notice the signs of growth within yourself. And, on the next Imbolc, the fully grown plant will help you reflect on where you were and where you are now.

Overall, the ritual will keep you mindful of your journey and your growth so that:

1.You wouldn't neglect yourself.

2.You wouldn't make the mistake of undervaluing your work and the effort you've dedicated to your journey.

Divination

Divination is the practice of seeking knowledge. It could be about the future or the present and about a major life decision or a feeling you've struggled with. You could even practice divination for someone, although it's important to get their full consent.

So, with divination, the possibilities are endless. What you need to remember is to be as specific as you can. When you ask someone for help, you would tell them what you want help with and how they can help, right? With divination, it's the same thing. You can't ask a deity or the universe for specific answers if you're not giving them a specific problem.

Specificity aside, how you practice divination is completely up to you. There are many ways and methods, so it's all about what makes you feel comfortable.

Tarot

Tarot cards are a great way to practice divination. They're fun, easy to use, and the medium allows for answers that don't require much interpretation.

You'll Need:

- Tarot deck
- Your cleansing method of choice

Instructions

1. Cleanse your deck and your space before you do your reading.
2. Ground yourself and find your center.
3. Hold the cards between your hands, channel your energy into them, and ask the cards your question.
4. Shuffle your cards until you feel satisfied.
5. Fan out the cards and choose the one you feel drawn to.
6. Pull out the card without flipping it over or turning it around and place it face down on the surface in front of you.
7. Flip your card right or left side up to reveal it.
8. Note the card's position (inverted or upright), read up on its meaning, and reflect on the answer you received.

Additional Information

- There are various types of spreads, from the three cards representing your past, present, and future to the 10-card Celtic cross, which delves deeper into questions.

Fire Scrying

Scrying is the act of looking deep into an object or a space to attain a trance-like state and connect with the answers or visions you're looking for. Fire is a great way to do that, especially on Imbolc, because it's when the element's influence is strong.

You'll Need:

- A candle or a fire

Instructions

1. Prepare a clear and safe area for yourself and ensure it's free of distractions. Cleanse your space, turn off your phone, and take care of any responsibilities that may break your focus.

2. Ground yourself through breathing exercises, meditation, yoga, or your method of preference.

3. When you feel ready, light your fire, and sit in front of it.

4. Take deep, slow breaths as you gaze into the fire. Don't put pressure on yourself to do it the right way. You'll know it's right when it is, and it will come to you naturally. Until then, simply look at the fire. Rest your eyes where it feels right, and see how the fire tongues dance and flicker. Note its colors and how it moves with the air around it. Listen out for the sound of the burning flames.

5. As you relax and grow more comfortable starting into the fire, you'll feel more and more ready to initiate this step. Connect with the energy of the fire and draw it towards you.

6. Keep your eyes, ears, and mind open to any visions, sounds, or thoughts you experience. Don't get distracted and start chasing ideas and thoughts. Remain present and mindful. Even if you decide to explore a thought that comes to you, do so by choice and because it feels right and not because you can't help it.

7. You should spend as much or as little time as you want in front of the fire. Stay in tune with your body and mind, and they will tell you when it's time to end the session. You'll either feel satisfied or a tad uncomfortable and distracted.

8. Toward the end of the session, look away from the fire and take a few moments to calm down and, once more, ground yourself. Show gratitude to your fire and the energies, spirits, or deities you've asked for help. Then, put out the fire/candle.

Additional Information

- Scrying can be done using any shiny object. You can use a water surface, a crystal ball, crystals with reflective surfaces, and the list goes on.

- If you're planning on scrying more than once, start keeping track of the messages that come to you. After each session, jot down your notes in a notebook. With time, you may start seeing certain repetitions and patterns.

A Brigid-Aided Divination

If you are interested in working with Brigid, this next divination ritual relies heavily on the help of the goddess.

You'll Need:

- An altar for Brigid
- A red candle
- Candle/Match

Instructions

1. Set up an altar for the goddess. You can use your Brigid doll, bed, and cross, among other items.

2. Ground yourself and find your center before speaking to Brigid.

3. Light the candle, greet Brigid and invoke her presence. You don't need any special words. Your sincerity is enough.

4. Stay mindful of your internal environment as you note how the goddess responds to you.

5. As you start noticing Brigid's presence around you, thank her for responding to you. Then, ask her your question. Be as specific as you want and give her as many details about what you need help with as you need to. If you have an idea of the solution, share that with her.

6. After you've finished talking to the goddess, thank her and then, when it feels right, blow out the candle.

7. Pay attention to your feelings and surroundings in the following days. Remember that the goddess won't turn the sky red and split the earth in half to send you a message.

She will subtly communicate with you. It could be a sighting of an animal, a plant, or an angel number. It could also be through a feeling or an experience. Remember to keep your mind and heart open and trust that your answer will come.

Baths

Just as Imbolc is a time to cleanse your space and your mind, it's also a time to cleanse and tend to your spirit and energy. Spiritual baths can help you relax on a spiritual level. They can also help cleanse you of negative energy and rejuvenate your energy reserves.

Now, all baths are done in the same way. The effects, however, vary depending on the herbs and ingredients used. So, to start, we'll discuss the method first.

General Instructions

1. It doesn't make sense to cleanse your spirit and energy in a dirty tub or a cluttered bathroom. So, prepare by cleaning your bathtub and organizing the space around it.
2. Figure out what you want from your bath - healing, energy, cleansing, etc. This will help you set the scene for your bath. Let your intuition guide you throughout this preparation process.
3. If you'd like to do something specific while bathing, figure it out to prepare for it, whether by buying a bathtub tray or clearing out a spot for it.

Some people are more vision-oriented. They like to have things like candles and flower petals all around them.

Others are more smell-oriented, so they burn essential oils or incense.

And others are sound-oriented, so they like to have their phone, tablet, or laptop nearby to pick up their music.

There's no rule on engaging all your senses either. It's all up to you and what relaxes you most.

1. Prepare your environment, then turn on the hot water and let it fill the tub. Add your salts and, in a cheesecloth, put your herbs of choice, tie the cloth, and let it steep. You can

also add your herbs directly into the water, but the cloth saves you the effort of collecting the leaves afterward.

2. Once the water has cooled down to your preferred temperature, it's time for you to soak.

Healing Bath Recipe

- Two generous handfuls of Epsom salt or pink Himalayan salt (cleansing)
- Lavender (calming)
- Chamomile (healing)
- Orange blossoms (relaxing)
- Rosemary (cleansing)
- Rose petals (relaxing)

Rejuvenating Bath Recipe

- Eucalyptus (refreshing)
- Mint (energizing)
- Jasmine (mood-boosting)
- Meadowsweet (mood-boosting)
- Dandelions (refreshing)

Chapter 10: Poems, Prayers, and Blessings

While Imbolc is for everyone, it has a special value for writers and poets. Not only is it the beginning of the spring - arguably the most beautiful season, but it is also tied to Brigid, a poet's goddess and muse.

Since Brigid is the goddess of poetry and wisdom, writing is a wonderful way of celebrating Imbolc and honoring the goddess.

Throughout the years, there have been poems written about Imbolc and Brigid. Not just that, but prayers and blessings too.

This chapter is all about poems, prayers, and blessings. It's dedicated to those who would like to recite a few verses in Brigid's honor and those interested in composing their own poems.

Poems

These next few poems are from a collection published by Jill Hammer in the Journal of Feminist Studies in Religion.

Imbolc

'Imbolc' gets off to a rather tragic start as the author doesn't shy away from describing the sense of despair, weakness, and hopelessness that she experiences during winter. It's a very relatable piece for those who experience hormone imbalances or Seasonal Affective Disorder during winter.

"Easier
if once having given birth
the new fawn straggled off to Eden
so much harder
to carry her with
her stick legs
over snowfields
if there were a brook
a fig left lying in the snow
a trickle of sap from a tree
to make the journey easier
o lady of the well of life
pity one who bears herself
through cold winter
Show yourself
though you dwell beneath frozen water
tap the ice until it breaks."

In this poem, the author calls upon Brigid to break the veil of winter and show herself. The poem starts with the author describing herself as a fawn and comparing her state during winter to that of a newborn deer. She starts pleading for Brigid to aid her by shattering the winter.

The author likens herself to a newborn fawn in the first and second stanzas. She also likens her emotional state in winter to the fawn's near-impossible journey from the land of the ice and snow to an Eden-like place. She wishes that spring would come soon, but like the fawn that journeys on weak legs, she too must travel across the metaphorical snowfields.

In the third stanza, she wishes for the slightest signs of spring and life to hold her over until she crosses the fields. She hopes to see a brook, a fig, or the faintest trickle of sap.

In the fourth and fifth stanzas, she outright calls for Brigid, the lady of the well of life. She asks the goddess to take pity on her as she tries to survive the bleakness of winter. She pleads for strength at first, but then she invokes the goddess's presence and asks her to break winter's hold.

The Feast of Brigid

This is a much brighter poem than the one before. It's a celebration of the coming of spring and of the role that Brigid plays in it.

"The red-haired girl draws milk
in a pail from the earth.
The earth is a spotted cow
with teats that are geysers
and anthills and rotten logs.
The red-haired girl
strokes and strokes
the dark soil.
When the milk rises in spurts
she catches its arc of white froth
to give out to visitors.
At the gate of the farm
the world holds out its hand,
while in a field rimed with frost
the first snowdrop toddles from the ground."

In this poem, the author celebrates spring and Imbolc with a set of beautiful imagery that likens the earth to a cow and Brigid to the red-headed girl that provokes the cow to release milk - a symbol for spring.

The poem opens with a red-haired girl milking the earth into a bucket. The red-haired girl here could easily be a symbol for Brigid herself. Overall, the image introduced in the stanza is unusual, but it's attention-grabbing, thought-provoking, and allows the author to elaborate in the next stanza.

In the second and third stanzas, the author elaborates on the first stanza by explaining that the world is a spotted cow and that the earth's features are its teats. Meanwhile, the red-headed girl continues to stroke the soil - just like Brigid brings the spring to its people.

In the fourth and fifth stanzas, milk erupts from the earth, and the girl catches it in her bucket. She then gives it to the people of the world who have gathered around the farm where the girl is.

The poem ends with a description of a snowdrop growing in a snow-covered field just as milk erupted from the earth. This part further confirms the theory that Brigid is the red-haired girl.

Prayers and Blessings

As a rule of thumb, the best prayers are the ones said and spoken from the heart. Of course, Brigid loves a good verse, but not at the cost of your authenticity. Ultimately, a verse is only a pretty vessel for what's truly important, which is the essence.

You can memorize and repeat prayers and blessings and still mean them with all your heart. This is why we will include and discuss a few of those. However, as you recite them, don't forget to do so with intention.

A Prayer of Thanks

"We welcome the season of Brigid
She who protects our hearth and home.
We honor and thank her
for keeping us warm as we eat this meal.
Exalted One, bless us and this food,
and protect us in your name."

This is a simple prayer that you can recite alone or with your family members. You can also recite bits and pieces of it as you go about your day or as you notice the subtle signs of spring.

A Prayer for the Coming of Light

"Blessed Brigid, shine your light
Bring us warmth from your fire,
And healing from your holy well."

This, too, is a simple prayer that you can say to invoke Brigid's presence and her strength. It can come in handy during tough times when the winter seems endless. It also doubles as a nice prayer of gratitude and a celebration of Brigid's strength when uttered during Imbolc and in spring.

How to Write Your Own Poem

Writing your own poem is a unique and wonderful way to express your feelings about Imbolc and Brigid. Poems can also be quite a special offering for the goddess.

Now, most people believe that it's hard to write poetry. The truth is, it's simple once you forget about all the pressures, rules, and judgments that come with doing any creative work.

So, take a moment to connect with yourself and think about an aspect of Imbolc that you feel drawn to – or the one that you love the most. Once you have that, you can flesh it out by exploring it even further. Perhaps, think about your favorite scenes in nature, your favorite aspects of Brigid, and why you like these things. What do they mean to you?

As you're exploring the premise of your Imbolc poem, try to incorporate all of your senses. Jill Hammer prodded her readers' imagination by invoking an image in' The Feast of Brigid. This made her poem much more vivid and interesting because it engaged our sense of sight. You can also focus on the smells, sounds, and even textures that you note during this time to draw a whole portrait.

When you've finished brainstorming, sit down, and let your feelings and intuition guide you. You can write a line a day or a poem a day, as long as you feel what you're writing and are not tapping a keyboard or scribbling on a paper.

Although, if you haven't written before, you might need to write a lot without "feeling" until you get the hang of writing. Once you're comfortable enough with the imagery and the phrasing, you'll be relaxed enough to let your feelings guide your writing.

That's all there is to it. And remember to write from the heart and try not to judge your writing. This is a form of expression. It's an act of love, and it can only thrive in a safe environment.

Conclusion

For pages and pages, we have explored all the aspects of Imbolc, from its earliest origins to its connection with Brigid. We have also included poems and prayers that can be recited to celebrate the event. And while there are no more words to say, the truth is, this book hasn't come to an end yet. In fact, it never will.

This book is about the physical, psychological, and spiritual aspects of Imbolc and Brigid, and these are not limited topics. They're ever-growing and ever-evolving.

With every person who reads this book, every scholar and researcher who explores the Celtic culture, traditions, and history, and every individual who celebrates Imbolc and Brigid, our collective knowledge of Imbolc grows.

Whether it is through new archeological evidence found, new spiritual experiences, spells, rituals, or even dishes, every person adds pages upon pages to this book. So, while this is a conclusion, think of it as a conclusion to only the part written by us.

Every pagan who celebrates Imbolc is writing down parts right now. It's time for you to start writing your part, too. So, take the information from this book, but don't stop there. Delve deeper within yourself, reflect on what you've read, and ask questions. Direct your hunger and curiosity toward exploring what Imbolc means to you and what it could mean to you.

Before you know it, you'll be creating your own rituals and spells. You'll start having your own traditions and dishes. You'll be able to start a conversation with, "I don't know about you, but Imbolc for me is about..."

And, for some of you, maybe it will come to you as a slow realization that Imbolc is not your festival. That's perfectly fine, too. What you celebrate doesn't define you as a human or as a pagan. Perhaps you feel more connected to a different festival. Perhaps you feel connected to none of them.

At the end of the day, all festivals are human-made. We give them meaning. So, now, it's up to you to find out what Imbolc means to you. Have a beautiful journey, and blessed be.

Here's another book by Mari Silva that you might like

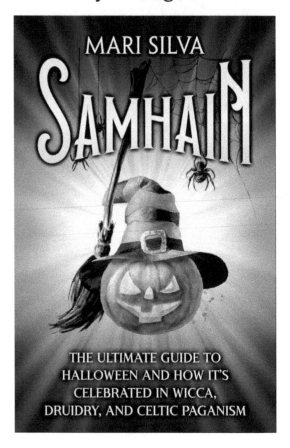

Your Free Gift (only available for a limited time)

Thanks for getting this book! If you want to learn more about various spirituality topics, then join Mari Silva's community and get a free guided meditation MP3 for awakening your third eye. This guided meditation mp3 is designed to open and strengthen ones third eye so you can experience a higher state of consciousness. Simply visit the link below the image to get started.

https://spiritualityspot.com/meditation

References

9 Thyme Magical Properties and Spiritual Uses. (2021, October 27). Angelical Balance. https://www.angelicalbalance.com/spiritual-protection/thyme-magical-properties/

Angelica Spiritual Meaning And Magical Uses. (n.d.). Sentientmetaphysics.Com. https://sentientmetaphysics.com/angelica-meanings/

Barbara. (2016, January 15). How to make a Brigid Doll (Straw Doll). Colorful Crafts. https://colorful-crafts.com/how-to-make-a-brigid-doll-straw-doll/

Bauer, E. (n.d.). Flourless Lemon Almond Cake. Simply Recipes https://www.simplyrecipes.com/recipes/flourless_lemon_almond_cake/

Bible Gateway passage: John 8:12 - English Standard Version. (n.d.). Bible Gateway. https://www.biblegateway.com/passage/?search=John%208%3A12&version=ESV

Bible Gateway passage: Leviticus 12 - New International Version. (n.d.). Bible Gateway.https://www.biblegateway.com/passage/?search=Leviticus%2012&version=NIV

Bible Gateway passage: Luke 2 - New International Version. (n.d.). Bible Gateway. https://www.biblegateway.com/passage/?search=Luke%202&version=NIV

Blanchard, T. (2021, May 22). 10 Spiritual Benefits of Bay Leaves (For Attracting Abundance & Positivity). OutofStress.Com. https://www.outofstress.com/spiritual-benefits-of-bay-leaves/

BRIGID. (2019, May 30). Goddess Gift. https://www.goddessgift.com/goddess-info/meet-the-goddesses/brigid/

Brigid: Lady of the Sacred Flame. (n.d.). The Goddess Circle., https://thegoddesscircle.net/visionary-writing/brigid-lady-sacred-flame

Brigid: Triple Goddess of the Flame (Health, Hearth, & Forge). (n.d.). Mimosa Books & Gifts. https://www.mimosaspirit.com/blogs/news/brigit-triple-goddess-of-the-flame-health-hearth-the-forge

Brigid's Cross: How to Make One for Imbolc * Wicca-Spirituality.com. (n.d.). Wicca-Spirituality.Com. https://www.wicca-spirituality.com/brigids-cross.html

BRIGID-unabridged. (2019, June 3). Goddess Gift. https://www.goddessgift.com/goddess-info/meet-the-goddesses/brigid/brigid-unabridged/

Build a Campfire. (n.d.). Smokey Bear. https://smokeybear.com/en/prevention-how-tos/campfire-safety/how-to-build-your-campfire

Candlemas, a festival of lights. (n.d.). Alimentarium.Org. https://www.alimentarium.org/en/fact-sheet/candlemas-festival-lights

Candlemas Day, Liturgical History : University of Dayton, Ohio. (2022, March 17). Udayton.Edu. https://udayton.edu/imri/mary/c/candlemas-day-liturgical-history.php

Celebrating Candlemas in Old Ireland - World Cultures European. (n.d.). Irishcultureandcustoms.Com. https://www.irishcultureandcustoms.com/ACalend/Candlemas.html

Chicken & Goat Cheese Pasta. (2017, May 2). Awesome on 20. https://awesomeon20.com/chicken-goat-cheese-pasta/

Collet, N. (2020, January 28). La Chandeleur. French Cultural Center. https://frenchculturalcenter.org/2020/01/28/blog-la-chandeleur-2020/

Corak, R. (2020, February 8). Phoenix Rising: Fire, Water, and Words: Divination with the Goddess Brigid. Agora. https://www.patheos.com/blogs/agora/2020/02/phoenix-rising-fire-water-and-words-divination-with-the-goddess-brigid/

Eason, C. (2016). 1001 spells: The complete book of spells for every purpose. Sterling.

Elm mythology and folklore. (2019, June 12). Trees for Life. https://treesforlife.org.uk/into-the-forest/trees-plants-animals/trees/elm/elm-mythology-and-folklore/

Every Rowan tree has a story. (n.d.). The Present Tree https://thepresenttree.com/blogs/tree-meanings/rowan-tree-meaning

Feb. 2 Christo-pagan Holiday Candlemas, Imbolc, Oimelc, Groundhog Day. (2017, February 27). Seminary. https://northernway.org/school/way/calendar/candlemas.html

Fleckenstein, A. (2014, November 5). 16 Healing Herbs For The Most Amazing Bath Of Your Life. Prevention. https://www.prevention.com/health/health-conditions/a20472817/healing-herbs-to-use-in-a-bath/

Garis, M. G. (2021, March 15). How To Make a Home Altar That Honors Whatever Energetically Empowers You. Well+Good. https://www.wellandgood.com/how-to-make-altar-home-design/

Green, M. (2018, April 3). Sigils: Barcodes for your Brain. Atheopaganism. https://atheopaganism.wordpress.com/2018/04/02/sigils-barcodes-for-your-brain/

Guardian staff reporter. (2000, October 28). The witching hour. The Guardian. http://www.theguardian.com/theguardian/2000/oct/28/weekend7.weekend3

Hammer, J. (2006). Imbolc poems. Journal of Feminist Studies in Religion, 22(1), 75–82. https://doi.org/10.1353/jfs.2006.0009

Hart, A. (n.d.). 3 Ways To Welcome The Warmth Of Spring This Imbolc. The Traveling Witch. https://thetravelingwitch.com/blog/2018-1-15-3-ways-to-welcome-the-warmth-of-spring-this-imbolc

History.com Editors. (2018, April 5). Imbolc. HISTORY. https://www.history.com/topics/holidays/imbolc

Imbolc. (n.d.). Taracelebrations.Org. https://www.taracelebrations.org/celebrations/imbolc

Imbolc / Candlemas. (2021, October 4). The Goddess and the Greenman. https://www.goddessandgreenman.co.uk/imbolc-candlemas

Imbolc - Symbols and Symbolism. (2021, August 25). Symbol Sage. https://symbolsage.com/imbolc-symbols-rituals/

Imbolc Divination Ritual. (2017, February 1). Tess Whitehurst. https://tesswhitehurst.com/imbolc-divination-ritual/

Imbolc: Traditions, Rituals, and Herbs for the pagan Holiday. (n.d.). HERBSTALK. http://www.herbstalk.org/1/post/2021/01/imbolc-traditions-rituals-and-herbs-for-the-pagan-holiday.html

Info. (2020, February 11). Brigid: Survival Of A Goddess. Order of Bards, Ovates & Druids. https://druidry.org/resources/brigid-survival-of-a-goddess

Irish American Mom. (2021, January 31). Explore the Origins of the Ancient Celtic Festival of Imbolc. Irish American Mom. https://www.irishamericanmom.com/explore-the-origins-of-the-celtic-festival-of-imbolc/

CPSIA information can be obtained
at www.ICGtesting.com
Printed in the USA
BVHW061019160223
658644BV00003B/247

9 781638 181750